PHILOSOPHICAL ANALYSIS

*An Introduction to Its Language
and Techniques*

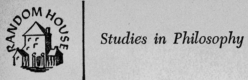

Studies in Philosophy

Consulting Editor:
V. C. CHAPPELL
The University of Chicago

PHILOSOPHICAL ANALYSIS

An Introduction to Its Language

and Techniques

by

Samuel Gorovitz *and*

Ron G. Williams,

IN COLLABORATION WITH

Donald Provence *and*

Merrill Provence

Random House · New York

THIRD PRINTING, NOVEMBER 1966

© 1963 by Samuel Gorovitz and Ron G. Williams
© Copyright, 1965, by Random House, Inc.

Library of Congress Catalog Card Number: 65–23334

MANUFACTURED IN THE UNITED STATES OF AMERICA

BY H. WOLFF, NEW YORK

Preface

Students beginning the study of history, literature, or physics have for the most part a roughly accurate idea of the nature of the subject matter they are about to confront. So it is with most fields. But students beginning the study of analytic philosophy have in general no idea at all what sort of discipline they are about to encounter. This lack of knowledge presents the instructor with an additional burden—one which is not easy to overcome. For the question of the nature of philosophy is itself a philosophical issue, which can be handled properly only when the students have—or perhaps are in the process of developing—some competence in philosophy. It is in the interest of advancing the development of such competence that this book was written.

The book was conceived during the course of an informal seminar on the teaching of philosophy organized by a group of Stanford graduate students. Part of the purpose of this seminar was to develop a rather detailed syllabus for the kind of introductory philosophy course that the members of the group believed they would like to teach. The consensus was that a beginning student should be given the opportunity to study a few basic philosophical problems in depth. It was decided that treatment of a few problems in depth could best be accomplished if the student were first given a concise introduction to the language of modern philosophy. No adequate written material for such an introduction was available.

This book is thus aimed at what the authors consider to be a specific need. We intend the book to provide the materials for a program of familiarization with the language and techniques of analytic philosophy, for students who have had no prior acquaintance with the discipline.

No attempt has been made to write a comprehensive survey of any sort. The topics that are included in this volume were chosen as being most relevant to the type of problem the authors wish to treat in their own courses. However, most of the topics discussed are so basic a part of modern philosophical analysis that they should be relevant to many different types of courses. In addition, we have attempted to include material that will help the student avoid what, in our experience, are the mistakes most commonly made by beginning students in philosophy.

This book provides no final word, and is no substitute for solid philosophical inquiry. Its purpose will be defeated if it is viewed as a compendium of philosophical method. Moreover, there is a serious danger inherent in the very nature of this book; any compact presentation of techniques and distinctions can, merely by its existence, give the impression that the problems of the discipline in question can be met simply by drawing upon a previously developed arsenal of procedures. Yet any such impression of philosophical inquiry is grossly in error. In fact, the distinctions and techniques described here, like all those in philosophy, arose out of confrontation with substantive issues, and were developed in the light of new problems. Yet to justify the distinctions we discuss by presenting an historical account of their development would defeat the purpose for which the book was conceived. We have, therefore, tried to motivate the development of the material in a natural way, but the major task in this respect lies in the hands of the instructor.

The various sections of the book are, insofar as possible, independent of one another. Where there is dependence, the relevant sections are cited. Thus, sections may be omitted or used in a different sequence at the option of the instructor.

The authors wish to acknowledge their indebtedness to the Philosophy Department at Stanford University for encouragement, advice, and material support in connection with this project. We wish also to thank the other members of the seminar, Marcia Muelder, Hugh Petrie, Terry Parsons, David Howell, and John Wallace, for their help in planning this book and for their criticisms of it. Michael Rohr was very helpful in the preparation of the bibliography. Professor Vere Chappell, as the publisher's advisor, provided valuable encouragement and evaluation throughout. Finally, our thanks are due to the many people in various fields who have provided constructive suggestions for the improvement of the manuscript.

Introduction

Philosophy is a discipline relatively free of technical language and specialized methods. Whereas the problems of modern physics, for example, can be appreciated only by those trained in advanced mathematics and experimental techniques, many of the most fundamental problems of philosophy can be stated in rather simple terms.

There are, however, certain concepts which find their primary use in philosophical discourse, and there are certain techniques—particularly those of symbolic logic—which are commonly employed by philosophers. This book is designed to acquaint beginning students in philosophy with the most important of these concepts and methods. A mastery of the material presented here should enable the student to progress more rapidly in his study of philosophy and to treat on a deeper level the philosophical questions he encounters. Such mastery can, of course, be gained only by a careful reading and rereading of the sections which follow.

The authors have attempted to give an impartial presentation of certain key terms and procedures—that is, a presentation which does not express a particular philosophical position. But this attempt is bound to fail, at least at some points, because virtually no inteesting discussion of a basic concept is noncontroversial, nor does any method have the approval of all philosophers. Therefore, we cannot overemphasize the point that this book does not provide any final word on philosophical method. To treat the book as a philosophical dictionary, or as an authoritative discourse on methods of analysis, can only lead to trouble. No list of techniques is a substitute for careful analysis and uninhibited thinking. Hence, the intended use of this book is as a starting point for a painstaking examination of the problems of philosophy—an examination which, if pursued with diligence, will surely lead to a reappraisal of the material presented here.

Contents

PHILOSOPHICAL ANALYSIS

*An Introduction to Its Language
and Techniques*

I

Elementary Logic

1. Arguments, Validity and Truth

We may consider logic to be an analysis of the structure of reasoning. We encounter reasoning in the form of arguments. An argument, considered from the viewpoint of formal logic, is a set of sentences, one of which purports to be a conclusion that follows from the others. Thus

A
- (1) All men are bipeds.
- (2) Edgar is a man.
- (3) (Therefore) Edgar is a biped.

is an argument in which line A(3) is the conclusion that follows from lines A(1) and A(2). If we know A(1) and A(2), we can deduce that A(3) is true. Lines A(1) and A(2) are called premises; line A(3) is called the conclusion.

Consider the following three lines:

B
- (1) All men are bipeds.
- (2) George is a man.
- (3) (Therefore) Rover is a biped.

Here, too, we have an argument, which resembles A in form. But this time we notice something strange. The purported conclusion, line B(3), does not follow from the premises at all. Even if we know B(1) and B(2) to be true, we can still deny B(3). So B, like A, is an argument, but B, unlike A, is not a good argument. Its conclusion does not follow from its premises, and we therefore call the argument invalid.

In any argument, the lines with which we begin, and from which the conclusion is supposed to follow, are called premises. We call them premises because we assert the conclusion on the assumption that they (the premises) are true. Thus, I may know that no one in San Francisco is seven feet tall, and that John Jones is a five foot New Yorker. Still, I can assert that if it *were* true that all San Franciscans are seven feet tall and that John Jones lives in San Francisco, then it would follow that John Jones is seven feet tall. The argument would look like this:

C
(1) All San Franciscans are seven feet tall.
(2) John Jones is a San Franciscan.
(3) (Therefore) John Jones is seven feet tall.

Argument C, like argument A, is valid; that is, the conclusion follows from the premises. The premises are said to imply or to entail the conclusion. But C, unlike A, has false premises. Thus, C(3) is a valid conclusion, because it is the conclusion of a valid argument, yet C(3) is not true. Hence we see that a sentence can be a valid conclusion and still be false. For, to say that a sentence is a valid conclusion is to say only that it must be true *if* the premises of the argument are true. The notion of a valid conclusion is thus a derivative notion, which makes sense only in terms of the notion of a valid argument. That is, a conclusion is valid only

Now let us consider the word 'and'. We can use it to join any two sentences into a third sentence. We will symbolize 'and' by '&'. Thus if 'P' and 'Q' are abbreviations for sentences, so is the single sentence symbolized as 'P & Q'. What can we say about the truth value of 'P & Q'? Consider the sentence 'It is raining and it is Tuesday'. This sentence is true only in case it *is* raining *and* it *is* Tuesday. Otherwise the sentence is false. We can show this with a truth table—the table for conjunction.

P	Q	P & Q
T	T	T
T	F	F
F	T	F
F	F	F

Here there are four rows, one for each possible combination of truth values for P and Q.

We call '&' a sentential connective, since with it we are able to connect sentences and make new sentences. Similarly, although we do not use '~' to *connect* sentences, we call '~' a connective, since we can make new sentences with it. '&' is a two-place connective— we use it between two sentences; '~' is a one-place connective—we use it with one sentence, such as 'P' or 'P & ~Q'. If we wish to negate 'P & ~Q', we must first put parentheses around the sentence we are negating and write '~(P & ~Q)'. This is to avoid confusion with '~P & ~Q'. Construction of the truth table for '~P & ~Q' will show that the truth conditions for '~P & ~Q' are different from the truth conditions for '~(P & ~Q)'. Thus the sentences are different, and must be distinguished.

Now, we can make new sentences in many ways.

Starting with 'P' and 'Q', we can form, for example, '~P', 'Q & ~P', '~P & ~Q', and '~(P & ~Q)'. It is a simple matter to construct truth tables for any of these sentences. Consider '~(P & ~Q)'. Here, we see that the sentence in question is a negation of the form '~R', where 'R' represents 'P & ~Q'. Thus, when we have all the possible truth values for 'P & ~Q', we can easily determine the truth values for '~(P & ~Q)'. Further, we see that 'R' is a conjunction of two components, 'P' and '~Q'. Since we know the truth table for conjunction, we can readily determine the truth values for the conjunction 'P & ~Q', if we know the values for the components 'P' and '~Q'. We will begin with a column for 'P' and one for 'Q'. We first add a column for '~Q', according to the truth table for negation. Next we combine the values of 'P' and '~Q' in another column according to the rules for conjunction. Finally, we obtain the values for '~(P & ~Q)' by applying the rules for negation to the values in the column for 'P & ~Q'.

P	Q	~Q	P & ~Q	~(P & ~Q)
T	T	F	F	T
T	F	T	T	F
F	T	F	F	T
F	F	T	F	T

This table shows us the truth conditions for '~(P & ~Q)'. It shows us that '~(P & ~Q)' will be true in every case except when 'P' is true and 'Q' is false. Thus, only if it is raining but the day is not Tuesday is it false that 'It is not the case both that it is raining and it is not Tuesday'.

We may now consider three more connectives. We

symbolize 'or' by 'v', and call this connective the disjunction sign. Thus 'It is raining or it is Tuesday' can be symbolized 'P v Q'. The truth table for disjunction is:

P	Q	P v Q
T	T	T
T	F	T
F	T	T
F	F	F

Here we note that a disjunction is true if both disjuncts 'P' and 'Q' are true. Thus, it is an *inclusive* sense of disjunction that is symbolized by 'v'. This sense is illustrated by, e.g., a sign above a door saying 'Salesmen or Messengers'. Clearly, in this case, a man who was both a salesman and a messenger would be permitted to enter. Notice the contrast with the more common *exclusive* sense of disjunction, illustrated by the father who says, "We will go to the movies or we will go on a picnic." Here the statement is intended to rule out the possibility of doing both.

The next connective we will introduce is '→'. It will be helpful, at least at first, to think of 'P → Q' merely as an abbreviation for '~P v Q'. Both expressions, then, will have the same truth table:

P	Q	~P	~P v Q	P → Q
T	T	F	T	T
T	F	F	F	F
F	T	T	T	T
F	F	T	T	T

We can see, by comparing this table with that given above for '$\sim(P \& \sim Q)$', that 'P → Q' is equivalent to '$\sim(P \& \sim Q)$' as well as to '$\sim P \lor Q$'.

Our main reason for introducing this connective is that 'P → Q' reflects at least one important feature of English sentences of the form 'If P then Q'. Such sentences—for example, 'If it is raining, then I will stay home'—are called *conditional* sentences. The sentence following 'If' (in this case, 'it is raining') is called the *antecedent*, while the sentence following 'then' (in this case, 'I will stay home') is called the *consequent*. The feature of such sentences reflected by '→' is that it is a basic part of the meaning of a conditional sentence that, if the antecedent is true and the consequent is false, then the entire conditional sentence is false. Thus, using the example above, if it is in fact raining, but I do not stay home, we would say that my statement—if it is raining, then I will stay home—was false. We can see that the second row of the table for 'P → Q' reflects this feature, since 'P → Q' is false when 'P' is true and 'Q' is false.

We may thus think of 'P → Q' as a symbolization of the English sentence form 'If P then Q', just as 'P ∨ Q' is taken to symbolize 'Either P or Q'. We will read 'P→Q' as 'If P then Q', and we will call 'P' the antecedent and 'Q' the consequent. One may be tempted to say that, if it is true that if P then Q, then we may say that 'P' implies 'Q'. For, if we say that a sentence 'P' implies a sentence 'Q', we mean that 'Q' follows from 'P'—that if 'P' is true then 'Q' must be true (cf. III, 1, B).[1]

Serious difficulties arise, however, if we try to interpret 'P → Q' as giving an adequate characterization of either 'P implies Q' or 'If P then Q'. Consider the first row of the truth table. Here, 'P → Q' is given as

[1] (Chapter III, Section 1, under B). This method of referring to other portions of the book will be used throughout.

true if 'P' and 'Q' are each true. If we were to accept this truth table as an adequate characterization of implication, then we would have to hold that any true sentence implies any other. Thus, according to the truth table, 'Plato was a Greek' would imply 'General Motors makes Chevrolets'. This seems undeniably strange, for we tend to think of a sentence of the form 'P implies Q' as true only when there is some connection between the antecedent and the consequent (in addition to the fact that they are both true).

In defense of interpreting '→' as 'if . . . then . . .', on the other hand, one can argue that the strangeness of saying that the above conditional is true results simply from the peculiarity of any conditional whose antecedent and consequent are unrelated. It would be at least as strange to hold that the conditional is false.

More serious difficulties arise when we turn to the third and fourth rows of the table. Consider the following conditional sentences:

(i) If Dionysius was born in 335 B.C., then Dionysius was born before 335 B.C.

(ii) If Dionysius was born in 335 B.C., then Dionysius was not born in 1950.

(iii) If Dionysius was born in 335 B.C., then Dionysius was born before 334 B.C.

(iv) If Dionysius was born in 335 B.C., then Dionysius was born in 330 B.C.

Now, assuming that Dionysius was born in 330 B.C., sentences (i)-(iv) all have false antecedents, and sentences (ii) and (iv) have true consequents. According to the truth table for '→', all four sentences are true because they all have false antecedents. Yet, only (ii) and (iii) are true. We can represent this discrepancy as follows:

According to the truth table for '→', sentences (i)-(iv) would be true as follows:

According to our intuitive understanding of conditionals:

A. (i) F → F : T
    (ii) F → T : T
    (iii) F → F : T
    (iv) F → T : T

B. (i) is F
    (ii) is T
    (iii) is T
    (iv) is F

This shows that '→' does not serve as an adequate characterization of all conditional sentences in ordinary language. Moreover, it shows that no connective given by a truth table could possibly work completely for implication, since (i) and (iii) would both be represented by the same row of any truth table as would (ii) and (iv), yet intuitively we know that (i) and (iii) differ in truth value, as do (ii) and (iv). Nevertheless, even though conditional sentences in English cannot be dealt with satisfactorily by truth-functional connectives, we shall use the connective '→', bearing in mind its limitations, to symbolize conditional sentences, since it does adequately reflect the fact that a conditional with a true antecedent and a false consequent is false.

Finally, we introduce the connective '↔' for equivalence or co-implication (sometimes called the "biconditional connective"). 'P ↔ Q' is an abbreviation for '(P → Q) & (Q → P)'.

P	Q	P ↔ Q
T	T	T
T	F	F
F	T	F
F	F	T

With reservations similar to those discussed for '→', we may take '↔' to symbolize the English phrase 'if and only if'.

To review: We have five connectives:[2]

not	~
and	&
or	v
if . . . then . . .	→
. . . if and only if . . .	↔

Now consider the symbolization of some simple sentences.

If you come, I won't drive.

'P' for 'You come.'
'Q' for 'I will drive.'

$$P \rightarrow \sim Q$$

If taxes are lowered and labor doesn't strike, then and only then will prices drop.

'P' for 'Taxes are lowered.'
'Q' for 'Labor strikes.'
'R' for 'Prices will drop.'
$$(P \& \sim Q) \leftrightarrow R$$

It is raining and it is not raining.
$$P \& \sim P$$
It is raining or it is not raining.
$$P v \sim P$$

Let us compare the truth tables for these last two sentences.

[2] Some writers use different symbols, for example: not, '—'; if . . . then . . . , '⊃'; if and only if, '≡'.

P	~P	P & ~P		P	~P	P v ~P
T	F	F		T	F	T
F	T	F		F	T	T

We see that 'P & ~P' is false, no matter whether 'P' is true or not. It is always false, because it is a contradiction. This is revealed by the truth table, which shows only F's in the column under 'P & ~P'. We agree that any sentence which has only F's as possible truth values will be called a *logically false* sentence—or a *contradiction.* 'P v ~P' on the other hand is aways true, no matter whether 'P' is true or not. We call 'P v ~P' a *logically true* sentence—or a *tautology.* Of course, not all true sentences are tautologies, and not all false sentences are contraditions.

We may now introduce the notion of consistency. We say that a set of sentences is consistent if no contradiction follows from it. Thus the set:

$$(1) \ \ P \to Q$$
$$(2) \ \ R \to \ \sim Q$$
$$(3) \ \ P$$
$$(4) \ \ R$$

is an *inconsistent* set of sentences because, as we can see from the truth tables for implication and conjunction:

(a) If 'P implies Q' is true, and 'P' is true, then 'Q' is true; and

(b) If 'R implies ~Q' is true, and 'R' is true, then '~Q' is true; and

(c) If 'Q' is true and '~Q' is true, then 'Q & ~Q' is true.

So sentences 1-4 imply 'Q & ~Q', which is a contradiction, and the set 1, 2, 3, 4 is thus inconsistent.

The notions of logical truth, logical falsity, tautology and contradiction have a wider application than is indicated here. What we have developed so far is a *partial* analysis of these notions. We may say, for example, that *if* 'P' (where 'P' might stand for a sentence of the form '(Q & ~R)→ S', or for any other) has a truth table in which every entry in the P-column is T, *then* 'P' is logically true. But the converse is not true. It does not follow from the fact that 'Q' is logically true, that 'Q' has such a truth table. Consider the sentence 'All brothers are brothers'. This sentence, although logically true, has no sentential connectives; thus, abbreviating this sentence as 'P', the only truth table for it is:

$$P$$
$$T$$
$$F$$

To analyze such sentences as this, we would need a much more powerful set of techniques. A small part of these techniques will be considered next.

II

Predicate Calculus and Sets

1. Predicate Calculus

The concepts and symbols introduced thus far do not allow us to reflect, in logical symbolism, the grammatical structure of simple sentences, such as 'All brothers are male siblings'. The general claim exemplified by this sentence is that all things having a certain property (that of being a brother, in this case) also have another particular property (that of being a male sibling). To symbolize such a sentence merely by calling it 'P' leaves the details of its internal structure inexplicit, and it is often this structure that determines the role of the sentence in arguments.

In what follows, the concepts and techniques for exhibiting the logical form of simple sentences will be developed, so that we will have a more powerful method for the analysis of sentences and arguments.

As an example of an obviously valid argument, consider:

> All Athenians are wise.
> Callias is an Athenian.
> Callias is wise.

A. As a first step in symbolizing this argument, we replace the name 'Callias' with 'c'. We shall use lower-case letters near the beginning of the alphabet to denote particular individuals; such terms are called *individual constants* (or merely *constants*). Constants need not stand only for proper names such as 'Callias'. We might, for example, let the constant 'd' stand for the phrase 'the wisest man in Athens'.[1]

B. The sentence 'Callias is wise' consists of a subject ('Callias') and a *predicate* ('is wise'). We will symbolize predicates by upper-case letters. In this case, let us replace 'is wise' by the *predicate symbol* 'W'. We will adopt the convention of writing the constant denoting the subject of predication immediately after the predicate symbol, so that 'Callias is wise' will be symbolized by 'Wc'.

It is often true that a particular sentence can be symbolized in several different ways. As an example, consider:

Callias is wise and Callias is an Athenian.

This sentence can be symbolized in at least two ways:

Wc & Ac.
Bc.

Here 'A' stands for 'is an Athenian', and 'B' for the compound predicate 'is an Athenian and is wise'. Which of these symbolizations of the original sentence is chosen will depend on the context in which it is to be used.

The predicate 'is wise' is called a *one-place* predicate because its predicate symbol is followed by one individual constant. Some predicates are two-place—for

[1] Phrases like 'the wisest man in Athens', which describe an individual person or object uniquely, are called 'definite descriptions'.

example, 'loves'. 'John loves Mary' may be symbolized by 'Ljm'. And, of course, there are higher-place predicates, such as 'lies between' in the sentence 'Point *a* lies between points *b* and *f* ' (symbolized by 'Babf').

Note that verbs are not the only words that can be symbolized by predicate symbols (as the word 'predicate' might lead one to expect). Adverbs, adjectives and prepositional phrases may all be symbolized by predicate symbols. Consider, as an example, the sentence 'Callias talks with Plato in the Academy'. We can treat everything after the word 'Callias' as a predicate and symbolize the sentence by 'Tc' (i.e. 'T' stands for 'talks with Plato in the Academy'). On the other hand, we may treat the predicate as a two-place predicate, 'talks in the Academy with'. In this case, the sentence would be symbolized by 'Acp' (here 'A', of course, stands for 'talks in the Academy with'). In general, a one-place predicate may be constructed from a two-place predicate by filling one of the places in the latter with a constant (as 'Plato' was added to the predicate 'talks in the Academy with' to form the one-place predicate 'talks with Plato in the Academy').

C. Consider the symbolization of the following sentences:

> Callias is wise.   Wc.
> Socrates is wise.   Ws.
> Aristophanes is wise.   Wa.

The form or pattern common to these expressions may be indicated by introducing *individual variables*, such as 'x' in the expression 'Wx'. (We shall use lower-case letters near the end of the alphabet for variables.) The variable 'x' does not denote any particular individual; it merely indicates the place which a constant, denoting some particular individual, may occupy.

D. In addition, a variable may be thought of as corresponding to a pronoun in ordinary language. Since Callias is wise, we may truly say:

(1) There exists someone, such that he is wise.

In symbolizing (1), we must make use of a variable, since the 'he' in (1) does not refer to any specific person, only to *someone*. Therefore, we begin the symbolization of (1) as follows:

(1a) There exists an x such that x is wise.
(1b) There exists an x such that Wx.

Finally, we introduce the *quantifier* '($\exists$x)' to stand for 'There exists an x':

(1c) ($\exists$x) (Wx)

(Note the use of parentheses to set off the quantifier from the rest of the sentence.)

Of course, it makes no difference which variable we use; (1) could just as well have been translated by '($\exists$y) (Wy)'.

The quantifier '($\exists$x)' is also read as 'for some x' or 'there is at least one x'.

Next, consider the sentence:

(2) Everything in the universe is red. That is,
(2a) For every thing, it is red.

We introduce the quantifier '(x)' for 'For all x', and the predicate symbol 'R' for 'is red'. Then (2) may be symbolized by:

(2b) For every x, x is red.
(2c) (x) (Rx).

(Here again 'y' could have been used in place of 'x'.)

The quantifier '($\exists$x)' is called the *existential* quantifier; '(x)' is called the *universal* quantifier. Other quantifiers are used by symbolic logicians (such as one standing for 'There exist exactly two things . . .'); but since these special quantifiers can be defined in terms of the two introduced above, no more will be said about them here.

E. Following are some examples of the translation of English sentences into the symbolic logic notation just introduced. The following predicate symbols and their corresponding English predicates will be used:

> Ax: x is an Athenian
> Cx: x is a Cretan
> Wx: x is wise
> Sxy: x is smarter than y

> (1) All Athenians are wise.

That is,

> (1a) For every thing, if it is an Athenian, then it is wise.
> (1b) (x) (Ax → Wx).

One may be tempted to translate (1) by:

> (1c) (x) (Ax & Wx).

But (1c) is clearly incorrect, for its English translation is 'All things are Athenians and are wise', which has not at all the same meaning as (1).

> (2)   Some Athenians are wise.
> (2a) There is at least one thing such that it is an Athenian and it is wise.
> (2b) (∃x) (Ax & Wx).

In the case of this second example, it would be *incorrect* to write:

> (2c) (∃x) (Ax → Wx),

because (2) is true only if there exists at least one wise Athenian, whereas (2c) may be true even if there are *no* wise Athenians. This can be seen by referring back to the truth table for implication and noting that 'P → Q' has the same truth table as '~ P v Q'. Since these two expressions are equivalent, we may replace (2c) by:

(2d) ($\exists$x) (~ Ax v Wx).

Now (2d) means that there exists something which is either *not* an Athenian or which *is* wise, so that (2d) is true so long as there is at least one thing which is not an Athenian. Thus, (2d), which is equivalent to (2c), can be true even when there are *no* wise Athenians, and it is clear that (2c) is not the correct translation of (2).

(3) All Athenians are smarter than all Cretans.

(3a) For all x and for all y, if x is an Athenian and y is a Cretan, then x is smarter than y.

(3b) (x) (y) ((Ax & Cy) → Sxy).

The third example illustrates the use of more than one quantifier; note also the ample use of parentheses to make (3b) unambiguous.

(4) Some Athenians are not wise.

This sentence may be symbolized in two ways. First consider it as a denial of (1).

(4a) It is not the case that all Athenians are wise.

(4b) ~ ((x) (Ax → Wx)).

Or we can paraphrase (4) by:

(4c) There is at least one thing such that it is an Athenian and it is not wise.

(4d) ($\exists$x) (Ax & ~ Wx).

Actually, it can be shown that (4b) and (4d) are equivalent in the sense that each follows logically from the other.

F. Finally, we shall symbolize the argument with
   which this section began:

> (I)   All Athenians are wise
>   Callias is an Athenian
>   ∴. Callias is wise.
> (Ia) (x) (Ax → Wx).
>   Ac
>   ∴. Wc.

The argument is clearly valid, because if it is true of
all individuals that, if they are Athenians, then they are
wise, then it is certainly true of any particular individual, say c, that if c is an Athenian, he is wise. The second premise tells us that c is indeed an Athenian.
Therefore, c is wise.

But not all arguments are so transparent, and it is
necessary to specify exactly and in detail what sort of
inferences can be legitimately made. This is done by
means of a set of rules usually called rules of inference.
A typical rule of inference is:

From '(x) (Hx)' infer 'Ha', where 'H' is any predicate, simple or complex, and 'a' is any individual constant.

Such a rule would allow us to deduce 'Rc' (i.e. 'Callias
is red') from '(x) (Rx)' (i.e. 'Everything is red').

To specify an adequate set of rules is too lengthy a
task to be undertaken here. The important points to
note about rules of inference are the following: These
rules allow us to transform a set of sentences (premises) into another sentence (a conclusion), with the
guarantee that, if the premises are true, the conclusion
cannot be false. That is, if an argument is constructed
so that the conclusion follows according to the rules of
inference, we are assured that the argument is valid.
Specifying the rules of inference gives content to the

phrase 'follows logically'. To assert that 'P' follows logically from 'Q' is to assert that a string of sentences can be exhibited, beginning with 'Q' and ending with 'P', such that each member of the string follows from one or more of the preceding members according to a rule of inference.

We are now in a position to state, very briefly, part of what is involved in constructing a predicate calculus.

To establish such a system of symbolic notation, we must first specify a vocabulary and give the rules for constructing sentences using this vocabulary. This entails listing those symbols that can be used as individual constants, one-place predicate symbols, two-place predicate symbols, and so on. Then rules are framed that state which strings of symbols are to be allowed as *well-formed*—that is, which are of a form that makes sense (such as 'Wc') and which are not (such as 'cƎW'). Second, the rules of inference are given. As noted above, they specify how one sentence can be inferred from another sentence or set of sentences.

It is important to note that these rules may be specified without any reference to the notion of truth, or to English words for which the symbols stand. That is, we may consider how a sentence such as 'Wc' can be combined with other sentences, what its role is in various arguments, and whether or not it is well-formed, without considering it as standing for some English sentence and without considering its truth or falsity.

The first kind of rule merely picks out some symbols as usable and some strings of symbols as allowed. The rules of inference may be thought of as telling us how to transform some strings of well-formed sentences into other well-formed sentences.

Such rules are called *syntactical*. Syntax is the study

of the form of certain groups of symbols abstracted from any questions about their content. In the preceding sections, we have closely related our remarks about logic to the English language, even introducing the symbols '&' and 'v' as standing for 'and' and 'or'. This is because the important use of logic for our purposes is in symbolizing English sentences and determining the validity of arguments. But it should be emphasized that logic proper is a purely formal study of the relations between certain abstract and uninterpreted symbols, and is independent of any particular natural language. Once we relate the symbolic notation to a natural language, by interpreting the symbols (as we did when we gave '&' the meaning of 'and'), we can raise questions of meaning and truth. If we ask about the meaning or truth of some particular expression, we are in effect asking a question about the subject of that expression. If, however, we ask questions about the general theory of meaning and truth, then we are dealing with questions of *semantics* (cf. VI, 8).

Often a formal system of logic is used to study a particular language or segment of language. In that case we must specify, in addition to the above rules, certain informal rules of translation from the formal language to the natural language (for example, English); i.e. such rules as that 'W' stands for 'is wise'. And further, we must specify what entities the variables range over and the constants denote.

Once all this is done, we have at our disposal a very powerful tool for the analysis of languages, arguments and concepts.

2. Sets

The notion of a set is, intuitively, the notion of a collection of things of one sort or another. Words often

used synonymously with 'set' are 'class' and 'collection'.
Examples of sets are:

> the set of all wise men,
> the set of chessmen owned by Jones,
> the set of kangaroos over twenty feet tall,
> the set of all positive odd integers,
> the set of letters in the Greek alphabet.

The examples illustrate that sets may have a finite or
an infinite number of members, and that the members
may be concrete physical objects or abstract entities
like numbers. Note that even though the members of
a particular set may be physical objects, the set itself is
not another physical object, but an abstract entity.
Note, also, that a set may be empty; that is, it may have
no members. Such is the set of kangaroos over twenty
feet tall.

The Greek letter 'ϵ' is used to stand for the concept
'is a member of'. Therefore, '$a\epsilon B$' is to be read 'a is a
member of (the set) B'.

If we wish to enumerate specifically the members of a
set, we enclose the names of its members in brackets;
thus, '[1,2,3]' names the set composed of the integers
1, 2, and 3. If B = [1,2,3], it is true that $1 \epsilon B$. The number four, however, does not belong to B, and this may
be indicated by writing '$4\notin B$'—i.e. '$\notin$' means 'does not
belong to'.

We can employ some of the symbols and concepts
of predicate calculus by observing that there is a close
connection between sets and properties. An object has
a certain property if, and only if, the object is a member of the set of objects having that property. The set
of all Athenians can, therefore, be characterized as the
set of all x such that x is an Athenian (Ax). Call this
set 'Θ'; we write:

$$\Theta = [x|Ax]$$

(Here '[x|Ax]' is read 'the set of all x such that x is an Athenian'). We know that c∈Θ (where 'c', as above, denotes Callias).

Many sentences that can be translated into the notation of predicate logic can be equally well symbolized using the notation of set theory. 'All Athenians are wise' may be written, for example:

(1) $(x) (x \in \Theta \rightarrow x \in \Omega)$,

where Θ = [x|Ax] and Ω = [x|Wx]. A partial English translation of (1) is:

For all x, if x belongs to the set of Athenians, then x belongs also to the set of those who are wise. (Where 'x' ranges over human beings.)

Two sets, A and B, are *equivalent* if and only if they have *exactly the same members*. Symbolically:

$$A = B \leftrightarrow (x) (x \in A \leftrightarrow x \in B).$$

In a trivial sense, A is equivalent to A, since it is obviously true that

$$(x) (x \in A \leftrightarrow x \in A).$$

We speak of a set A as being a *subset* of another set B when every member of A is also a member of B. We use the symbol '⊂' for 'is a subset of'. Symbolically:

$$A \subset B \leftrightarrow (x) (x \in A \rightarrow x \in B).$$

Thus, [1,2,3] is a subset of [1,2,3,4], but the converse is not the case. In a trivial sense, any set A is a subset of itself, since for any set A it will be true that

$$(x) (x \in A \rightarrow x \in A).$$

Thus [1,4,7] is a subset of [1,4,7]. We now introduce the notion of a *proper subset,* so as to distinguish between those subsets of a given set A which are not equivalent to A, and A itself. We introduce the symbol '$\subseteq$' for 'is a proper subset of'. Thus:

$$A \subseteq B \leftrightarrow (x) \ (x \epsilon A \rightarrow x \epsilon B) \ \& \sim (x) \ (x \epsilon B \rightarrow x \epsilon A).$$

We may say, for example, that the set of husbands is a proper subset of the set of men, and is equivalent to the set of married men.

III

Further Logical Notions

1. Important Terms

What follows are some remarks about the meanings and uses of a few key words and phrases, which occur sufficiently often in philosophical writings to deserve special attention. These words are discussed here because, although they are often used outside the context of logic, they constitute an important part of the technical vocabulary of logical analysis.

A. 'IMPLY', 'INFER' AND 'ENTAIL'

These are three closely related words which can easily be misused. Roughly, the distinction between the first two is that *people* infer whereas *sentences* imply. Thus, we may say:

(1) Jones infers 'Q' from 'P'.
(2) Sentence 'P' implies sentence 'Q'.

(1) means in part that Jones considers it to be the case that 'Q' follows from 'P'. But Jones can be in error; he can infer incorrectly. In contrast, 'P' cannot incorrectly

imply 'Q'—either 'Q' follows from 'P' or it does not, and to say that 'P' implies 'Q' is simply to say that 'Q' does follow from 'P'. Thus the phrase 'incorrectly implies' has no meaning.

We may characterize inference, therefore, as a relation between a *person* and two sets of sentences (premises and conclusion); to infer is to accept a conclusion on the basis of a set of premises, it is to conclude. (We use 'infer' also in a derivative sense, to mean 'conclude from the *fact* that . . .' instead of 'conclude from the *premises* that. . .' .)

Examples:

(3) Jones inferred from the first three premises that A does not equal B.

(4) Jones inferred from the fact that the sun was up that it was later than 5 A.M.

Implication, on the other hand, strictly construed, is a relation between two sets of sentences. Consider:

(5) 'All Athenians are wise and Callias is an Athenian' implies 'Callias is wise'.

(6) The fact that Callias is an Athenian and all Athenians are wise, implies that Callias is wise.

Unfortunately, the picture is a little more complicated than has yet been indicated, because there is a use of 'imply' in which *people* are said to imply.

(7) The speaker implied that war was imminent.

We may take (7) to be short for 'The speaker implied *by what he said* that war was imminent'. But even if we construe (7) to mean that it was the sentences used by the speaker rather than the speaker himself that implied the imminence of war, there is one further notable difference in the way 'imply' is used in (7). When we say that a person implied something, we don't always mean that what is implied follows logically from what he said; sometimes we mean that, in saying what he said, he suggested or hinted at some conclusion. In this sense, 'imply' has a meaning close to that of 'intimate'.

We have already seen that the truth-functional notion symbolized by '→' is not an adequate characterization of the notion of implication, in so far as 'P' implies 'Q' only when 'Q' follows from 'P'. Nonetheless, some writers refer to that truth-functional notion as implication, and read 'P → Q' as 'P implies Q'. In order, therefore, to eliminate the possibility of confusion about the use of the word 'implies', we shall henceforth speak of *entailment* as being the relation which holds between 'P' and 'Q' when 'Q' does follow from 'P'. Thus we shall take ''P' entails 'Q'' to mean that 'Q' does follow from 'P'.

B. 'PRESUPPOSE'

Closely related to 'imply' is the term 'presuppose'. Indeed, 'presuppose' may be used to mean the same thing as 'imply'.

But, in its most common use, it is *people* who presuppose. In this sense, 'presuppose' means to assume, or to take for granted the truth of some sentence without explicitly acknowledging or asserting that fact.

Examples:

> (8) When Smith argued that the senses provide us with accurate information about external physical objects, he was presupposing that such objects exist.
>
> (9) Most ancient Greek astronomers presup-

posed that all heavenly bodies moved in circular paths.

It is part of the philosopher's task to make as many of his presuppositions explicit as is feasible; sometimes those things taken most for granted are most in need of careful inspection.

This process of making presuppositions explicit cannot go on without limit, of course. No one expects a physicist to include reasons for supposing that the sun exists, in a paper on nuclear processes in the sun's corona, even though the scientist does presuppose the sun's existence.

C. CONTRADICTION AND CONSISTENCY

Two sentences are *contradictory* if and only if one is the negation of the other or is logically equivalent to the denial of the other. Thus, 'It is raining' and 'It is not the case that it is raining' are contradictory sentences. Their conjunction, 'It is raining and it is not raining', is a *contradiction*.

The term 'consistent' is predicated of sets of sentences. A set of sentences is *consistent* if and only if no contradiction can be derived from the sentences in the set. The sentences 'Callias is wise' and 'Socrates is an Athenian' are consistent. The sentences 'All Athenians are wise', 'Callias is an Athenian', and 'Callias is not wise' are *inconsistent* because from them can be derived the contradiction, 'Callias is wise and Callias is not wise'.

D. NECESSARY AND SUFFICIENT CONDITIONS

(1) If Carl won the 2-mile race, then Carl officially entered the 2-mile race.

(2) If Carl ran the 2-mile race in the fastest time ever recorded, then Carl won the 2-mile race.

These two sentences are chosen to illustrate the difference between *necessary* and *sufficient* conditions. The truth of 'Carl officially entered the 2-mile race' is a necessary condition for the truth of 'Carl won the 2-mile race'; that is, it is necessary to enter a race in order to win it. But clearly, it is not sufficient for winning a race that one enter it. Something more is required—namely, officially completing the course before any other contestant.

Consider (2). The truth of 'Carl ran the 2-mile race in the fastest time ever recorded' is a sufficient condition for the truth of 'Carl won the 2-mile race'; that is, it is sufficient to win a race that one run the race in the fastest recorded time. But it is not necessary, because it is possible to win a particular race and still not break any record.

When two sentences are connected by 'If . . . then . . .', the first sentence is called the antecedent and the second the consequent. We may generalize the remarks made about the example sentences by saying that the truth of the antecedent of a conditional sentence is a sufficient condition for the truth of the consequent. The truth of the consequent is, on the other hand, a necessary condition for the truth of the antecedent. Consider sentences (1) and (2) again. The truth of 'Carl won the 2-mile race', which is the antecedent in sentence (1), is a sufficient condition for the truth of 'Carl officially entered the 2-mile race', since no one can win a race in which he is not officially entered. And the truth of 'Carl won the 2-mile race', which is the consequent in sentence (2), is a necessary condition for the truth of 'Carl ran the 2-mile race in the fastest time ever recorded', since he could not have run the race in the fastest recorded time without winning.

In a bi-conditional sentence, '. . . if and only if . . .', the truth of either of the two sentences connected by 'if and only if' is a necessary *and* sufficient condition for the truth of the other. As an example, consider:

> (3) Joel is Martha's husband if and only if Martha is Joel's wife.

E. 'IS' AND 'SAME'

1. The verb 'to be' is used in at least three ways, which should be carefully distinguished.

First, note that 'is' may be used to indicate identity. The sentence, 'Callias is the wisest man in Athens' may be translated by 'c = d', where 'd' denotes 'the wisest man in Athens'. That is, Callias is identical with that wisest man. In the sentence 'Two plus two is four', 'is' again means 'is identical with'.

Second, 'is' may be used to predicate some property of an object. The 'is' of predication is illustrated by 'Callias is wise'.

Finally, we sometimes use 'is' to indicate the unqualified existence of something as in the sentence 'He is' (i.e. 'he exists'). In this case no property is predicated of the subject; we are merely claiming that the subject exists.

These distinctions are so straightforward that one may well wonder why they are made at all. The fact is that it is not always a simple matter to decide which way 'is' is being used, and it is sometimes easy to be misled by failing to make these distinctions. For example, the fact that 'is' can play these different roles can lead to confusion as to whether a particular statement is a factual claim or a definition. Suppose a moral philosopher says, "Pleasure is good." It may not be clear whether he is claiming that pleasure has the property of being good or that good and pleasure are identical (i.e. that they are one and the same property). It may even be that the philosopher in question is not sure which he means, and his arguments in support of the claim may take advantage of this ambiguity.

2. The word 'same' suffers from an ambiguity similar to that of 'is'.

'A is the same X as B' may mean that A is identical with B (here 'X' is a kind of thing, like 'man' in the following example). Example: 'Johnson and the 36th President of the United States are the same man'.

But often, of course, 'same' means something like 'similar in relevant respects'. If we say, "Jones and Smith have the same job," we mean that they both have the same kind of job—that they are both corporation lawyers, for example. We do not mean that they hold identically the same job.

The distinction to be made here can be put more precisely by noting that both claims used as examples can be paraphrased using the notion of a set. The first sentence says that the names 'Johnson' and '36th President of the United States' both denote a single member of the set of men. The second claim is that Jones and Smith both belong to a particular set of jobholders, in this case, the set of corporation lawyers.

In using 'same' in this second sense, to mean 'belongs to the same set', one must insure that it is clear what the relevant respects are in which the objects in question are said to be the same. The context of discussion will usually make this clear. For example, the claim that all brands of aspirin are the same would generally be understood to mean that they are all about equally effective in relieving pain, reducing fever, etc., not that they are all sold at the same price.

But it is often the case that it is not at all clear what is meant by a statement of the form 'A and B are the same' or 'A is like B'. This imprecision of 'same' and 'like' is emphasized in riddles such as the Mad Hatter's

famous question, "Why is a raven like a writing desk?".
Unfortunately, some philosophical statements turn out
to be riddles when they are not intended to be.

F. 'MUTUALLY EXCLUSIVE' AND 'JOINTLY EXHAUSTIVE'

The two terms, 'mutually exclusive' and 'jointly exhaustive', are predicated primarily of sets. The sets in a
given collection of sets are said to be *mutually exclusive* if and only if no two sets in the collection have any
member in common. Thus, the set of even positive integers and the set of odd positive integers are mutually
exclusive because no number belongs to both sets.

In any particular application of the concepts and
techniques of set theory, we have in mind a collection
of objects which can be members of the sets with
which we are concerned. That is, if we are discussing
real number theory, we will be interested in sets whose
members are real numbers. Or we may be discussing
sets whose members are men, factories, and so on. In
each case, we can define a *domain of discourse*—a collection of entities from which may be drawn the members of the particular sets under discussion. The sets in
a given collection of sets are said to be *jointly exhaustive* if and only if every member of the domain of discourse is a member of one or more of the sets in the
collection.

If we take as the domain the set of positive integers,
then the two sets of odd and even integers mentioned
above are jointly exhaustive. If our domain is the set of
positive real numbers, then those two sets are not
jointly exhaustive, because the number π, for example,
is a positive real number but not an integer.

The sets in a collection of sets may be jointly exhaustive without being mutually exclusive and vice versa.

As a final illustration, let the domain of discourse, D,
be defined by:

$$D = [A,B,C,D,E].$$

(1) The sets [A], [B], [C], [D], [E] are mutually exclusive and jointly exhaustive.

(2) The sets [A,B], [B,C], [D,E] are jointly exhaustive but not mutually exclusive.

(3) The sets [A], [B], [C,D] are mutually exclusive but not jointly exhaustive.

We often speak loosely of properties rather than sets being mutually exclusive, meaning that no object has both properties. For example, evenness and oddness (of numbers) are mutually exclusive properties.

G. UNIVERSALS AND PARTICULARS

The predicate calculus, as described above, rests on a distinction between individual constants or names and general terms or predicate symbols. This distinction is a reflection of the more basic philosophical distinction between *particulars* and *universals*.

Intuitively, a particular is any individual entity—any thing which can be given a proper name. Socrates, the number five, and the third manhole cover going east from Broadway on 42nd Street are each particulars.

But besides particular men, there is the general concept *man*, and besides honorable men there is *honor*. That is, there are general properties or concepts called *universals* which are or can be common to more than one particular. Redness is a universal; redness can be attributed to individual physical objects; the red particulars are instances of the universal, redness. Evenness (as a property of numbers), beauty, and honor are other universals. A universal may have no instances. Man is a universal concept which has many instances; unicorn, on the other hand, has none.

2. *Modal Logic*

In philosophy of religion, as elsewhere, one often hears it said of some claim not merely that it is true, but that it is *necessarily* true. Thus, for example, it is sometimes claimed that it is necessary that God exists. But too often such claims are obscure, and if we are to evaluate them successfully, we need a clear characterization of what such terms as 'necessary' and 'possible' mean.

As is the case with most words, the word 'necessary' is used in many different ways, and the different kinds of ways in which it is used reflect different senses or meanings which the word can have. Consider these examples:

(1) It is necessary that you renew your driver's license.
(2) Food, shelter, and clothing are necessary.
(3) It is necessary that today is Monday or today is not Monday.

There are two different senses of necessity exemplified by these examples. First, consider (1) and (2). Of course, it is not necessary in an unqualified sense that one renew an expired driver's license. It is only necessary if the licensee is to continue to drive legally. But one could give up driving, or drive without a license. Thus, (1) is really what we might call a conditional statement of necessity, since it is only *if* one is to continue to drive legally that license renewal is actually necessary. Similarly, (2) is implicitly conditional upon one's sustaining life. Yet the necessity of sustaining one's life might be denied, as in the case of one who wishes to starve to death in protest against an oppressive regime. Such a person might deny (2). But (3) is not conditional as (1) and (2) are. *Any* sentence of the form 'P v ~P' is simply necessary; there is no condition upon which the truth of (3) depends. Rather, 'Today is Monday or today is not Monday' is true, and necessarily true, because to deny it is to make a logical error—to assert something contradictory. Thus, we might say that whereas (1) and (2) are statements of conditional or practical necessity, (3) is a statement of *logical* necessity.

Just as we have distinguished between practical and logical necessity, we may distinguish between practical and logical *possibility*. For example, it is impossible in practice for a man to lift a one-ton block of stone. But it is not a logical impossibility—there is no contradiction in saying that a man lifts a one-ton stone. On the other hand, it is logically impossible for a man to lift a *spherical cube* of stone, because the notion of a cube which is also a sphere is a self-contradictory notion.

Philosophers, insofar as they are concerned with the notions of possiblity and necessity, are interested primarily in *logical* necessity and possibility. We shall therefore try to present a more formal characterization of these notions, bearing in mind that it is only the logical sense of possibility and necessity that this characterization is aimed at reflecting.

Let us begin by assuming that we understand what it means to say that some sentence 'P' is necessary, i.e., that it is necessary that 'P' is true. We can now define the notion of possibility in terms of that of necessity, saying that a sentence is possible if its denial is not necessary. We introduce '□' for 'It is necessary that' and '◇' for 'It is possible that'. Thus: '□ P' is equivalent to '~ ◇ ~P'. Similarly, the notion of an impossible sentence may be defined. 'P' is impossible if it is not possible, i.e., if '~ ◇ P'. But '~ ◇ P' is the same as '□ ~P'. So impossible sentences are necessarily false.

We may now state a few of the more important relationships which hold among sentences to which are prefixed the *modal operators* '◇' and '□'.

If 'P' is necessary, then 'P' is true. That is, '□ P' entails 'P'.

If 'P' is necessary, and 'P' entails 'Q', then 'Q' is necessary. That is, whatever follows from a necessary truth is itself a necessary truth.

If 'P' is possible, and 'P' entails 'Q', then 'Q' is possible. That is, whatever follows from a possible proposition is itself possible.

If 'P' is necessary, then 'P' is possible. That is, if a proposition is necessary, then it is surely possible.

The plausibility of these principles is apparent, and no arguments in support of them will be offered here.

We say that a sentence is *contingent* if it is neither necessary nor impossible. The relationships among the modalities of necessity, possibility, and contingency are summarized below.

If 'P' is	we write	or, equivalently	'P' is also	'P' is not	'~ P' is
necessary	□ P	~ ◇ ~ P	possible	contingent impossible	impossible
possible	◇ P	~ □ ~ P	—	impossible	—
contingent	~ □ P & ~ □ ~ P	◇ P & ◇ ~ P	possible	necessary impossible	contingent possible
impossible	□ ~ P	~ ◇ P	—	necessary possible contingent	necessary

We may now clarify this discussion of modal logic by characterizing the notion of logical necessity which we assumed above (p. 40) to be clear. We shall say that a sentence is necessary if and only if its denial is or entails a contradiction. Necessary propositions are thus of three kinds: (1) truths of logic, like 'P v ~P', such that their denial leads to contractions of the form 'P & ~P'; (2) analytic truths, like 'All male siblings are brothers', which are not obviously truths of logic, but the denials of which can nonetheless be reduced to obvious contradiction via substitution of expressions for synonymous expressions (cf. VI, 2); (3) some truths—such as 'If A caused B, then A did not happen after B'—the status of which is uncertain. Sentences of this third type are said by some to be synthetic *a priori,* but others wish to hold that though they are indeed necessary, it is because they are of the second type, and still others wish to deny that they are necessary.

We may now express the modalities of possibility and contingency in similar fashion. We say that a sentence is possible if its denial is not necessary. A sentence will be contingent when neither it nor its denial is necessary. Finally, a sentence is impossible if it entails a contradiction; that is, if it is the denial of a necessary sentence.

We now have an elementary and informal system of modal logic. How useful this system is in analysis of arguments involving modal notions will of course be a reflection of the degree to which the interpretation of necessity on which it depends corresponds to the actual meaning of the modal language in the arguments under consideration.

IV

Assertions, Sentences and Propositions

Philosophers typically are concerned in a number of ways with questions of truth. Thus, for example, in Chapter I we discussed the relationship between the truth of some sentences (the premises) and that of some other sentence (the conclusion) in an argument. Another philosophical inquiry about truth has to do with the meaning of the word 'true'. Thus one might ask what it means to say of some assertion that it is true. (Cf. IX, 8.) Still another question one might ask is "What is true?" But that question can be taken in at least two ways: (1) as an inquiry into what the facts about the world are—that is, an inquiry into which of the claims of physics, sociology, economics, etc. are true; or (2) as an inquiry into what *sorts* of things are true—that is, an inquiry into whether it is sentences, actions, assertions, or people that can have the property of being true. It is with the second question that we shall be concerned in this section. That question is one which must be answered, for if we do not know what kinds of entity can have truth value, we may not be able to tell whether or not some questions make sense, when they are of the form 'Is x true?'—e.g., 'Is Smith's action true?'.

The word 'true' appears in many contexts that are not of special concern to a philosopher interested in problems of truth. Consider a few examples: 1) John is true blue. 2) That material is true alligator, not a plastic imitation. 3) My husband has always been true to me. There is very likely some connection between these uses of 'true' and the concept of truth that philosophers have been interested in. But these examples are not typically of philosophical interest. The following conversation, on the other hand, contains a use of the predicate 'is true' in a context that might be used as a starting point for a philosophical examination of the concept of truth.

> Apprentice electrician: There is no point in going back to the truck for a voltmeter. I can check it with my fingers; 110 volts isn't going to hurt me.
>
> Journeyman electrician: That's true; but if it is 220 volts, the twenty foot drop to the ground may be a bit jarring.

As this conversation indicates, we often use 'true' as a sort of me-too expression; a short way to say what has just been said or to agree with what has just been asserted. Thus one might say that the kind of thing that can be true or false is *assertions*. But if this answer is to provide insight into the concept of truth, we must ask what assertions are. Are they sentences, or are they actions? It is sufficient for our purposes to note that sentences and actions are indeed different sorts of things and that therefore the claim that assertions are the

things that are true or false is subject to differing inter-
pretations.

Asserting is something that people *do;* so we might
say that assertions are a kind of action. But it is at least
counter-intuitive to say that actions are the sorts of
things that are true or false. We would not want to say
that every action—e.g., John's robbing of a bank—was
either true or false. We would want a way to distinguish those actions that can be true or false from those
that cannot. Thus it becomes clear that the claim that
assertions are the things that are true or false is not un-
problematical.

We have said that 'true' is often used to assert the
same *thing* as has been said, to agree with *what has
been asserted.* Perhaps we should have said that it is
the product of an act of asserting—what is *asserted*—
that is either true or false. Let us for the moment say
that sentences are what is asserted, and thus that it is
sentences that are either true or false. This seems to
give a clear answer to the second question about truth,
since it seems to be clear what sentences are. But consider this: How many sentences are there in the box
below?

A
> Peter is thirteen years old.
> Peter is thirteen years old.

Is there one sentence there or two? Philosophers concerned with language have settled this question by
making a distinction between sentence-*types* and sen-
tence-*tokens.* There are two tokens in the box, but only
one type. A written token is a collection of physical
objects, in this case bits of paper marked with ink and
arranged in a specified order with appropriate spacing.

A spoken sentence-token is probably best thought of as an event, a happening, of which people are usually made aware by vibrations in some physical medium. Consequently, I can show you the same written token many times, but a spoken token can never be reduplicated: each token is a particular object or event. Written tokens can be copied, and spoken tokens can be reproduced by a tape recorder or copied by a skillful mimic; but two written tokens, no matter how much they look alike, are still two tokens. A spoken token and a reproduction of it occur at different times and are two events, two tokens. But although the two tokens in the box are different tokens, they are obviously alike in many respects; so much so that we might often say that there is only one sentence in the box. The likeness of these tokens is often explained by saying that they instantiate, that is, are instances of, the same sentence-type, or that they are tokens of the same type. Sentence-types are not physical objects that can be located in space and time; thus it was misleading to say that there is one sentence-type *in* the box. There is only one sentence-type instantiated by the sentence-tokens which are in the box. The same sentence-type might also be instantiated in handwriting, or in italic type, and it might be instantiated orally; thus two tokens can differ a great deal and still instantiate the same type. All that is required for two tokens to be of the same type is that they are composed of the same words in the same language in the same order. Nonetheless, just how much two tokens can differ while instantiating one type is not always clear.

If 'thirteen' in the first token had been misspelled, we would probably say that the tokens still instantiated the same type. But a difference in one letter can be enough to assure that two tokens instantiate different types; consider:

B

> Charles is married to Jo*a*n.
> Charles is married to Jo*h*n.

But if it is sentences that are either true or false, is it sentence-types or sentence-tokens? If it is sentence-types that can be true or false, we might say that the type instantiated by the token 'Peter is thirteen years old' is true only at the time when Peter is actually thirteen years old. But fixing the type a token instantiates does not fix the reference of the terms in the token; that is, we do not know who Peter is, we do not know to whom the name 'Peter' refers. We have already said that tokens instantiating the same type may differ from one another in many ways; clearly they may be spoken or written at different times and by different people. Different tokens instantiating this same type may be used to refer to many different persons named Peter, only some of whom will be thirteen years old. Suppose tokens of this type appeared on the medical chart of Peter Smith, who is thirteen years old, and on the chart of Peter Brown, who is twenty years old. What then would we say of the truth of the type? In one case Peter is thirteen years old; in the other Peter is not. But we do not want to say that the same sentence-type is both true and false.

In discussing the possibility of types being true, we mentioned the idea of the reference of tokens; in fact, it was tempting to say that the token that referred to Peter Smith was true, while that which referred to Peter Brown was false. Let us see whether sentence-tokens provide a more satisfactory answer to the question of what sorts of things can be true or false.

We do not immediately face the same problem with tokens that we faced with types, since it is unlikely that

'Peter' in any one token would refer to different Peters.
A particular token is written or uttered in a particular
context, which aids in determining the reference of its
terms; for example, the token written on Peter Smith's
medical chart. But sometimes it is not possible to determine the reference of a particular token. Is the first
token in box A above true or false? That token was
used as an example, and as such it has no context
which aids us in establishing the reference of 'Peter'; it
was not written on someone's medical chart, nor
spoken at Peter Smith's birthday party. If we do not
know to whom 'Peter' refers, how can we decide
whether the token is true or false? Although we may be
convinced that 'Peter' does not refer to *more* than one
person named Peter, have we any assurance that 'Peter'
does refer to *anyone* named Peter? The person responsible for that token's being produced may not have had
any person named Peter in mind. If 'Peter' in this token
does not refer to anyone, what does it mean to say that
the token is true? We might well maintain that, even if
tokens are generally the things that are true or false,
some tokens are neither true nor false. This should not
be particularly surprising, since we began this discussion by talking about things that are asserted in an act
of assertion, and the first token in the box above was
not asserted, it was merely used in illustration. It may
still be the case that all asserted tokens are either true
or false.

At this point, it is well to reflect on the course of this
discussion. Because it seemed counter-intuitive to say
that actions can be true or false, we were led to say
that it is what is asserted—sentences—that can be true
or false. And because the question of the truth of a
sentence-type was complicated by the fact that tokens
of the same type can have different reference, we
turned to sentence-tokens. But is it any more plausible

to say that these collections of physical objects or events are true or false? Isn't it rather what these things *mean* that is important in discussions of truth? Suppose someone asserts ' 'P' entails 'Q' ' and also asserts 'P', expecting us to infer 'Q'. Isn't it going to be important whether the 'P' in ' 'P' entails 'Q' ' means the same thing as 'P' in isolation? Surely something must be the same in the two cases, in order that the entailment may hold. But *what* must be the same? The tokens are obviously different, and tokens of the same type can have different truth values. We want not only tokens of the same type, but tokens that mean the same thing, have the same reference, and therefore the same truth value. Because of the importance of meanings in such considerations, philosophers have sometimes said that logical relations hold among *propositions,* i.e., among the meanings of sentence-tokens, rather than among the tokens themselves, and that these meanings or propositions are the things that are true or false.[1]

If two English sentence-tokens mean exactly the same thing, then it is said that they are synonymous and express the same proposition. For example, we might say that 'Not every dog is white' and 'It is not the case that every dog is white' express the same proposition. Whereas the same sentence-type can be instantiated by tokens which have different meanings, the same proposition can be expressed only by tokens which have the same meaning, since a proposition is the meaning of a token. Further, one proposition may

[1] We do not directly discuss the claim that it is statements which are either true or false, since the word 'statement' has been ambiguously used in philosophical discussion. Statements have been taken to be acts of assertion, sentence-tokens, sentence-types, and propositions; but all of these notions have been discussed in this section. The same remarks apply to the word 'claim'.

be expressed by sentence-tokens in different languages. If an English sentence-token can be translated into German without change in meaning, then the English token and its German translation express the same proposition.

Tokens are particular objects or events, each token being spoken or written in a particular language and at a particular time. Propositions are not bound to any particular language; and they are timeless. That is to say, if propositions are what is true or false, and if some particular proposition is true now, then it always has been and always will be true. Note that while any one written token may instantiate only one sentence-type, it may express more than one proposition at different times. Imagine that we construct a letter by cutting sentence-tokens out of magazines and pasting them onto a sheet of paper. It is quite possible for one of these tokens to express a different proposition in the magazine from the one that it expresses in the letter—i.e. to have a different meaning in each case. But the only way we have of saying what proposition a sentence-token expresses is to produce another token in the same or a different language, that is synonymous with the first token—i.e. to point to another token that has the same meaning and thus expresses the same proposition. If propositions are what is true or false, then this one token might be said to express a true proposition in the magazine and a false one in the letter. On the other hand, if tokens are what is true or false, we will have one token which is both true and false, but at different times. We might say that the truth value of the token has changed, but this change has been made possible only by the fact that the token expresses first one proposition, then another. The truth values of the propositions expressed, however, have not changed.

Yet, there are difficulties inherent in asserting that it is propositions that are either true or false, because the concept of a proposition is not entirely precise. We have said that a proposition is the meaning of a sentence and that the sentence *expresses* the proposition. But consider the sentence 'It is cold out today'. If we say, once in winter and once again in summer, "It is cold out today," then presumably what we have said in the winter is true and what we have said in the summer is false. Yet the sentence seems to have the same *meaning* in both cases. If (1) the meanings are the same, (2) the propositions expressed are the meanings, and (3) the truth values apply to the propositions, then the truth values cannot differ. While still maintaining that it is propositions which have truth value, we can try to avoid this problem in at least two ways. We could deny that propositions are meanings after all. But then we would have to regard meanings and propositions as distinct entities, thereby raising problems concerning the relations between the meaning of a sentence and the proposition it expresses. The denial that propositions are meanings offers no insight into the claim that it is propositions that are either true or false. We could instead hold the view that propositions are meanings, but deny that the meanings are the same in the two cases referred to above. We would then hold that the meaning is adequately specified only when we specify time and location in each case. But this attempt is open to the objection that it is only because the sentence has the same meaning, whether it is spoken in summer or winter, that it is false in 100° summer heat, but true in 20° winter cold. That is, if the sentence had one meaning when spoken in winter and a different meaning when uttered in summer, it might express a true proposition on both occasions. On either of these proposed alternatives, we are still faced with the task—in general a troublesome one—of identifying the proposition expressed by a given sentence.

Even if, in the above example, we could specify what proposition was expressed, by expanding the sentence so as to include time and location, such a simple procedure will not usually succeed. Consider the sentence 'Salem is in Massachusetts'. If 'Salem' refers to Salem, Massachusetts, then the proposition expressed by the sentence is true. But if 'Salem' refers to Salem, Oregon, then the proposition is false. How can we expand the sentence to make clear what proposition is expressed? It is not appropriate here simply to fill in time and place co-ordinates, since in this case the truth value of the proposition does not depend on the time or place it is asserted. If we expand the sentence to 'Salem, Massachusetts is in Massachusetts', then we have specified the reference of 'Salem' and the proposition expressed is clearly true. But the original claim, that Salem is in Massachusetts, is contingent, while the proposed expansion of the sentence is necessarily true. Given the reasonable hypothesis that, if two sentences express the same proposition, then one is contingent if and only if the other is, the proposed expansion does not express the same proposition as the original sentence did and does not show which proposition was expressed by 'Salem is in Massachusetts'.

There are of course other ways in which we might specify the reference of 'Salem', in an attempt to determine what proposition is expressed by the original sentence, and yet preserve the contingency of the original sentence. Consider, for example, 'The Salem which was founded in 1626 is in Massachusetts'. If this sentence expresses the same proposition as the first, then the first expressed a true proposition and 'Salem' therein refers to Salem, Massachusetts. However, it seems to be a reasonable assertion that, if two sentences express the same proposition, then neither conveys more information than the other, nor contains any assertion that the other does not. But if this is so, we cannot hold that 'Salem is in Massachusetts' and 'The Salem which was founded in 1626 is in Massachusetts' express the same proposition. Even if true, the first conveys, for example, no information in regard to the founding date of any city. And the second, if we suppose the conditions of utterance to be normal, is used to assert in part that there is one, and only one, Salem that was founded in 1626; the first, under normal circumstances, cannot be thus used.

Of course, we have not shown that it is altogether impossible to expand a sentence so as to make explicit what proposition is expressed by the original sentence. Neither have we shown that there can be no other way to determine what proposition is expressed by a given sentence. What we have shown is that the specification of what proposition a sentence expresses is in general no simple matter. Yet, in order for the claim that it is propositions which are true or false to be enlightening, there must be some way of making such a specification.

Thus, the question of just what sorts of things are true and false has not been settled here. We shall follow the practice of speaking simply of sentences as true or false. But it must be remembered that, although this manner or speaking is here adopted for the sake of simplicity, the question of the vehicles of truth is a complex one indeed.

V

Extensional and Intensional Sentences

Aristotle said long ago that it was important to distinguish between voluntary actions and those that are not voluntary, because praise and blame are bestowed on those that are voluntary, but not on those that are not voluntary. This distinction is not always easy to make; in fact, our first attempts may seem to end in contradictions. Consider a simple example: Joan comes home two days early from a visit to her home town. The same night her husband, Conrad, comes home very late and finds that he has forgotten his key and is locked out. He knows that he can get in through the bedroom window and does so. Joan awakens to see a man starting to climb through the window. She reaches into the drawer by the bed, pulls out a gun, shoots and wounds Conrad. Did Joan shoot Conrad voluntarily? She says that she did not; she didn't know that it was Conrad, and there is no reason to suppose that she is lying. On the other hand she admits that she voluntarily shot the man crawling in the window. But surely Joan's shooting Conrad and Joan's shooting the man climbing through the window were the same action. Thus, by a simple inference, we can conclude that Joan shot Conrad voluntarily. Yet this directly contradicts Joan's honest claim, which she can support with good reasons. The way out of this difficulty lies in making a distinction between *intensional* and *extensional* sentences.

We begin by introducing several closely related terms that are commonly used in discussions of synonomy and related topics in philosophy of language. We may speak of the *sense* and the *reference* of a word or phrase. We may also speak of its *intension* and *extension* or, less commonly, of its *connotation* and *denotation*. It is important to note here that: (1) 'intension' and 'extension' as introduced here are not to be confused with 'intension*al*' and 'extension*al*' as introduced above; (2) 'intension', with an '*s*', is a technical term, not to be confused with the ordinary English word 'intention', with a 't'; (3) 'connotation' and 'denotation' are not used in philosophical contexts as they often are in English grammar books. With these cautions in mind, we may proceed.

In philosophical usage, 'sense', 'connotation', and 'intension' are roughly equivalent, as are 'reference', 'denotation', and 'extension'. To see what the distinction is between sense and reference, consider the following example: The morning star and the evening star are the same planet. Thus the phrases 'the morning star' and 'the evening star' both refer to the same object, i.e. they have the same reference, denotation, and extension. But 'the morning star' and 'the evening star' do not have the same meaning or sense, as can be seen from the following argument. If one wishes to know whether the morning star is identical with the morning star, he would need only to reflect on the logical structure of the sentence 'The morning star is identical with the morning star'. His evidence, if any, would be from logic rather than from astronomy (cf. VI). But consider the sentence 'The morning star is identical with the evening star'. The evidence for this sentence comes from astronomical investigation. No one could have discovered that these two phrases referred to the same planet simply by reflecting on the meanings of the phrases.

This difference in relevant evidence indicates that the two sentences differ in meaning. Yet they differ only in that the second has the phrase 'the evening star' substituted for one occurrence of the phrase 'the morning star' in the first. The obvious reason why the sentences differ in meaning is that the phrases differ in meaning, even though both refer to the same object. We might also have argued that these phrases differed in meaning while having the same reference, by noting facts like the following. A person may believe that Venus is the morning star without believing that Venus is the evening star, and yet be said to understand the meaning of both these phrases. Similarly, someone may hope to see 'the evening star' in his telescope without hoping to see 'the morning star'. Thus two words or phrases can differ in meaning while referring to the same object, and the meaning of a word or phrase is seen to be something different from the object to which the word or phrase refers. As mentioned above, we call the meaning of a word or phrase its *sense* or *intension,* and the object(s) to which the word or phrase refers its *reference* or *extension.* Words or phrases that mean the same thing, i.e. are synonymous, are called *intensionally equivalent;* words or phrases that have the same extension or reference are called *extensionally equivalent.* Our discussion of 'the morning star' and 'the evening star' has shown that phrases may be extensionally equivalent while differing in intension or meaning; if two terms are intensionally equivalent, however, then they must be extensionally equivalent.

So far, we have been speaking about words or phrases having intensions and extensions. But sentences, too, have meaning, and we must widen these notions to apply to sentences as well. We shall say that the intension of a sentence is its meaning—or in other words, the proposition it expresses. But what is the extension of a sentence? It is not clear that sentences refer to anything at all. Nonetheless, we say that the extension of a sentence is its truth value.[1] Thus sentences that express the same proposition are intensionally equivalent or synonymous, while sentences are extensionally equivalent if they have the same truth value. Note that the use of 'extension' in the case of sentences is somewhat different from its use for words or phrases. A connection between these two uses of 'extension' may be arrived at by reflecting that the extension (truth value) of the proposition expressed by a sentence depends in part on the extensions (references) of the phrases in the sentence.

We now summarize the above material graphically (p. 58). Note that if we consider meaningful sentences, (a) some sentences are called extensional (though all have extensions, i.e. all have a truth value), and (b) some sentences are called intensional (though all have intensions, i.e. all express propositions).

We may now proceed to the task of clarifying the distinction between intensional and extensional sentences.

In the discussion above, we touched on the relation between the extension or reference of a sentence (its truth or falsity) and the extension or reference of the

---

[1] This view, presented here for the sake of completeness, is derived from the writings of Gottlob Frege.

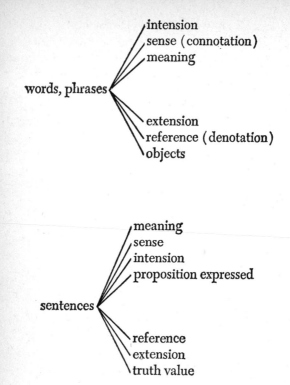

terms that are used to make up that sentence. For example, in order to determine whether it is true that
Peter is thirteen years old, one would have to determine at least (1) to which Peter the name refers, and
(2) whether that Peter is included in the extension of
the predicate 'is thirteen years old'—that is, whether
the predicate is true of Peter. Suppose that the person
to whom the name 'Peter' refers is the same person as
the oldest son of John. Then if we substitute the description 'the oldest son of John' for the name 'Peter' in
the sentence 'Peter is thirteen years old', the terms in
the resulting sentence 'The oldest son of John is thir-

teen years old' have the same reference as the terms in the original sentence. Furthermore, the two sentences have the same extension, that is, the same truth value. Sentences like these, in which one can substitute extensionally equivalent terms one for another without producing a sentence of a different truth value from the first, may be called *extensional* sentences. To consider some sentences that are not extensional in this sense, let us suppose that Peter has a limited knowledge of astronomy and that, while the following sentence is true:

> (1) Peter believes that Venus is the morning star.

This sentence is false:

> (2) Peter believes that Venus is the evening star.

Sentence (2) was obtained from sentence (1) by substituting for a description of Venus in (1) another description that refers to the same heavenly body. If these two sentences were extensional, in the sense discussed above, they would not then differ in their truth value. Instead, sentences like (1) and (2) may be called *intensional*.

Let us generalize on this discussion by offering a rule of thumb to aid in distinguishing intensional from extensional sentences by pointing out one respect in which intensional sentences are like one another and at the same time different from extensional sentences.

A. Let S be any sentence, and let R be any sentence which is obtained from S by substituting for any name or description in S any other name or description which refers to the same object. If for every such sentence R, S and R always have the same truth value, then they are extensional. But if there is any sentence R whose truth value differs from that of S, then S and R are intensional.

Note that it may be possible to make extensionally equivalent substitutions which do not change the truth value of an intensional sentence. For example, suppose that the following sentences are true:

> (3) Peter believes that Venus is the only planet whose diameter is 7,600 miles.
> (4) The oldest son of John believes that Venus is the morning star.

The fact that (3) and (4) have the same truth value as (1) does not show that these sentences are extensional. Rather we see that they are intensional because there is one sentence—sentence (2)—which can be obtained from sentence (1) or (3) or (4) by substituting terms that refer to the same object, yet the truth value of sentence (2) differs from that of (1), (3) and (4).

The failure of an extensionally equivalent substitution to preserve truth value is one mark of an intensional sentence. Let us consider another mark—the possibility that a name or description in a sentence may not refer to something in the world, even though the sentence is true.

> (5) Peter is looking for the planet which is 1,000 miles in diameter.
> (6) John hopes to ride Pegasus.
> (7) Peter needs a good text on astronomy.

Contrast these sentences with the following:

> (5a) Peter has found the planet which is 1,000 miles in diameter.
> (5b) There is no planet which is 1,000 miles in diameter.

(6a) John is not riding Pegasus.

(7a) Peter is reading a good text on astronomy.

Just as men could search throughout the middle ages for the Holy Grail even though there was probably no such object, so sentence (5) can be true even though (5b) is true. But sentence (5a) entails that there is a planet which is 1,000 miles in diameter; that is, it entails something which contradicts (5b). So (5a) and (5b) cannot both be true. Similarly, John can hope to ride Pegasus whether there is a Pegasus or not, whether the name 'Pegasus' refers to anything which exists or not. And we could not tell from the fact that Peter *needs* a good text on astronomy whether there was such a text or not. But if it is true that Peter *is reading* a good astronomy text, then such a text must exist. Let us generalize on this mark of an intensional sentence in another rule of thumb, which provides a sufficient but not necessary condition for intensionality.

B. Given a sentence S (not a statement of identity), containing names or descriptions $d_1, d_2, \ldots, d_n$; if it is not the case that either S or its negation ~S entails for *each* name or description d_i in S either that d_i does or that d_i does not refer to some object, then S is intensional.

Thus, (5a) is not shown to be intensional, because it entails that something exists to which the name 'Peter' refers and that, further, something exists which is referred to by the description 'the planet which is 1,000 miles in diameter'. And (5b) is not shown to be intensional because it entails that the same description fails to refer. But (5) *is* intensional, because neither it nor its negation entails either that the description refers or that it fails to refer. (6a) does not entail that 'Pegasus' does or does not refer, but since its negation does entail that both John and Pegasus exist, then (6a) may be extensional.

Rules A and B provide alternative rules of thumb in testing for intensionality, and there should thus be no conflict in result. Either rule, for example, will show that the following sentence is intensional:

(8) Peter hopes to be the first man on Venus.

Peter may hope that he will be the first man on Venus without hoping that he will be the first man on the evening star. And Peter could hope that he will be the first man on Venus even if there were no such planet as Venus. Thus, by both A and B, (8) is intensional. But if:

(8a) Peter is the first man to reach Venus.

then there must be something which he reaches. And if he is the first to reach Venus, then he is the first man to reach the evening star, the morning star, the only planet in our solar system whose diameter is 7,600 miles, etc.—whether or not he knows or believes that these descriptions all denote Venus. Thus, (8a) is not shown to be intensional by B, and is shown to be extensional by A.

Sentences about a person's beliefs, such as (1) and (2), are paradigms of intensional sentences; in fact, sentences about psychological phenomena generally provide the typical examples of intensional sentences.

In Chapter II, it was pointed out that the logical structure of such sentences as 'All bachelors are bachelors' cannot be adequately dealt with by propositional logic alone. Propositional logic is also inadequate to deal with the internal structure of intensional sentences, e.g.:

> (9) John believes that painting is a pleasant recreation.

However, the following consideration may lead us to try treating intensional sentences by methods similar to those of propositional calculus. Consider:

> (10) John believes that painting is *not* a pleasant recreation.

Since, typically, if (9) is true (10) will be false (and vice versa), we may be tempted to treat such expressions as 'John believes that . . .' and 'Peter hopes that . . .' as one-place sentential connectives, similar to 'It is not the case that . . .' . But these connectives, which we may call intensional, will differ from negation because they are not truth-functional; that is, we cannot construct for them a truth table which will enable us to compute the truth of 'John believes that P' on the basis of the truth of 'P'. That no such table is possible can be seen from consideration of sentences (1) and (2). 'Venus is the morning star' and 'Venus is the evening star' are both true, but sentences (1) and (2) differ in truth value even though each is the result of applying the same one-place connective to sentences with the same truth value. Since we are no better equipped to understand the structure of sentences using non-truth-functional connectives than that of intensional sentences, little is to be gained by treating expressions like 'John believes that . . .' as connectives.

Further, it should be noted that the methods of analysis provided by the predicate calculus are likewise not adequate to reveal the features of the internal structure of intensional sentences, such as we have been discussing.

If a sentence is extensional, then inferences of the following form are valid, according to the rules of inference of predicate calculus:

> The dog bites Jim.
> Jim is Joan's only son.
> Therefore, the dog bites Joan's only son.

But an inference of precisely the same form is invalid if one of the premises is an intensional sentence. Consider:

> Peter believes that $x = y$.
> $y = z$.
> Therefore, Peter believes that $x = z$.

Both premises of this argument can be true and still the conclusion be false (as exemplified by (1) and (2) above), and similarly with the argument with which we introduced this section. We cannot infer from 'Joan's shooting the man crawling in the window was voluntary' and 'The man crawling in the window was Conrad' that 'Joan's shooting Conrad was voluntary'.

Although we now have some tests for intensionality, it would be a mistake to assume that we can always tell easily whether or not a given sentence is intensional. Consider, for example:

> (11) John loves Mary.

It is open to question whether or not (11) entails that Mary exists. Moreover, if Mary is the bank teller, and John knows the bank teller but doesn't realize that she and Mary are one, it is open to question whether or not substitution of 'the bank teller' for 'Mary' in (11) will preserve the truth value of (11). Thus, on both tests, it is unclear whether or not (11) is intensional.

We have noted that intensionality is a mark of sentences about psychological phenomena. One might therefore suggest that (11) is intensional because it concerns love, surely a psychological phenomenon. But this would beg the question of whether or not sentences about psychological phenomena are all really intensional. To answer that question, the intensionality of sentences must be determined independently of whether or not they concern psychological phenomena.

In any case, not all sentences that are intensional by virtue of tests A and B are obviously sentences about psychological phenomena. Thus,

(12) It is possible that Venus is not the morning star.

(13) It is necessary that Venus is Venus.

are both true. But if we interchange the two terms which refer to Venus, we get:

(12a) It is possible that Venus is not Venus.

(13a) It is necessary that Venus is the morning star.

and both of these are false. Thus (12), (12a), (13), and (13a) are intensional by rule A. Yet they do not seem to involve psychological phenomena.

VI

The Analytic-Synthetic and *A Priori-A Posteriori* Distinctions

1. Introduction

The distinctions to be discussed below were first systematically set forth in the eighteenth century by Immanuel Kant, but they were implicit in the works of many of his predecessors.

It requires little reflection to convince oneself that the criteria we employ and the kinds of evidence we cite for the truth of particular claims vary markedly from case to case.

Suppose, for example, that we wish to discover whether the following claims are true:

(a) All animals are animals.
(b) The pear trees are in bloom.

In the latter case, one might well go to the place where the pear trees grow and look for blossoms, whereas the truth of the first sentence is evident merely upon an examination of its logical structure. The only evidence one might cite for (a) would be from a logic text, but the request for evidence seems out of place. The thing we do not do is go out in search of animals to see if they are animals.

To take a more interesting example, consider:

(c) God exists.

Traditionally, this claim has been supported or denied on widely divergent grounds. Some have insisted that (c) follows deductively from logically true premises; others that God's existence must be postulated to account for the world as we observe it to be; still others have held that because, in their view, (c) cannot be refuted or proved on the basis of the evidence of the senses, it is a meaningless claim.

These few examples are sufficient to suggest a host of philosophically interesting questions. What criteria of truth are relevant to the claims of theology or of physics? What kinds of evidence confirm the claims of natural science, or ethics, or the social sciences? And how is such evidence related to the corresponding claims? What sorts of things can be known by reason alone, without reference to sense experience? And so on.

The distinctions which follow were propounded not in order to answer such questions, but in an attempt to help clarify them and make them more precise.

2. *Analyticity*

(1) $(P \& (P \rightarrow Q)) \rightarrow Q$.
(2) Queen Elizabeth II is identical with Queen Elizabeth II.
(3) A brother is a male sibling.
(4) All brothers are males.
(5) Some bachelors are married.

The sentences above share this property: their truth or falsity can be determined by an examination of their logical form and perhaps the meanings of the words used to express them as well.

The first sentence is a tautology. The second has the logical form a = a and is thus logically true. By substituting in (3) for 'male sibling' its synonym 'brother', (3) can be reduced to a logical truth. Thus, the truth of (3) follows from the meanings of the words; that is, by substituting synonyms for synonyms, we can convert (3) into a sentence the form of which is obviously that of a truth of logic. The same is true of (4). Since brothers are male siblings, (4) is equivalent to 'All male siblings are males', which again has the form of a truth of logic. The meaning of the predicate in (4) is part of the meaning of the subject; (4) is a partial analysis of the term 'brother'. Finally, (5) is seen to be false once we consider the meaning of 'bachelor' and the logical form of the sentence.

Such sentences are said to be *analytic*.[1] Analytically true sentences are thus of two kinds—those [like (1) and (2)] which can be seen to be truths of logic, merely by inspection of their logical form, and those [like (3) and (4)] which can be seen to be logical truths by substituting synonyms for synonyms and then examining the logical forms of the resultant sentences. Analytically false sentences are those which are self-contradictory. As before, synonyms may have to be

---

[1] In Chapter II, some reasons were given for claiming that propositions rather than sentences are true or false. Thus, one might want to claim that it is propositions that are analytic or synthetic. This view is further motivated by the fact that criteria for analyticity depend heavily on word meanings and synonymy, so that sentences that have the same meanings (or express the same propositions) will be alike in analyticity. In this chapter, as throughout the book, we follow common usage in calling *sentences* analytic or synthetic. But, of course, the possibility remains open that it is the propositions expressed by these sentences that are analytic.

substituted for synonyms to make evident the fact that a sentence is self-contradictory.[2]

Another way to make the same distinction is to say that the denial of an analytically true sentence is self-contradictory.

All sentences which are not analytic are called *synthetic*. Some examples follow:

(6) Queen Elizabeth II was born in 1926.
(7) John has three brothers
(8) It is often the case that bachelors own sports cars.
(9) The Earth is flat.

Neither synthetic sentences nor their denials are self-contradictory. Their truth or falsity cannot be determined by word meanings and logical form alone. Crudely put, a synthetic sentence has an extralogical content, and we must look beyond the analysis of the meanings of the words involved to settle its truth value. To assert that a particular synthetic sentence is true is to assert that one of two mutually exclusive but logically possible states of affairs (described by the sentence and its denial) is actually the case.

3. *The* A Priori

Setting aside temporarily the analytic-synthetic distinction, we can divide all sentences into two groups, according to whether or not they can be known to be true or false without consulting experience. Sentences of the type that can be refuted or confirmed only by experience (i.e. on the basis of observation) are called *a posteriori*. They are to be distinguished from sen-

---

[2] Often 'analytic' is used for 'analytically true', i.e. often 'S is analytic' is intended to entail 'S is true'.

tences known to be true (or false) without empirical evidence; these latter are *a priori* sentences. Thus, an *a priori* sentence is such that we can conceive of nothing that would count as evidence against it.

Examples of *a posteriori* sentences are easily found.

(10) It rained yesterday.
(11) It looks like rain.
(12) It will rain tomorrow.

All these are of the type of claim whose truth (or probability of being true) is to be found only by consulting our experiences.

But consider the mathematical equation

(13) $5 + 7 = 12$.

What experience will refute or confirm (13)? If we put five apples into a basket, add seven more, and then count eleven apples in the basket, has (13) been refuted or cast into doubt? Clearly not. We will seek some physical explanation or counting error, and continue to consider (13) true. (13) is thus a paradigmatic example of an *a priori* sentence.[3]

4. *The* A Priori *Synthetic, Etc.*

We are now in a position to construct a table illustrating the four combinations of the above criteria, and the kinds of sentences that fall under them.

---

[3] In ordinary discourse we often use '*a priori*' to mean independent of some particular experience rather than totally independent of experience, as we are using it here. An example of this ordinary use is "He should have known *a priori* that she would get angry with him for breaking the date." That is, he should have known what her reaction would be prior to the actual *particular experience* of breaking the date.

Note too that *a priori* does *not* mean *before* experience, but *not based upon* experience. Of course, we can have no knowledge of any kind before we have had experiences.

	A Priori	A Posteriori
Analytic	I. P or not-P. All dogs are animals.	II.
Synthetic	III. Every event has a cause.	IV. The book is red.

Clearly, there are no *a posteriori* analytic sentences (group II) because analytic sentences are true by virtue of the meanings of their words alone, so that neither refutation nor confirmation by experience is possible. Therefore, all analytic sentences are *a priori* (group I).

Group IV comprises those sentences whose truth does not follow from word meanings and logical form, but from experience. Examples of such 'empirical' claims are, of course, easy to find. Particular observational and predictive claims of natural science, as well as the bulk of our everyday conversation, belong to this group.

As might be expected, the most controversial category is group III, synthetic *a priori* sentences. Sentences of this type are not merely analyses of words, nor are they true on logical grounds alone; they "say something about" the world of our experience, and yet they are known independently of empirical evidence. Leaving aside the controversy for the moment, we may justify the example given, as follows:

(14) Every event has a cause.

The negation of (14) is not self-contradictory, so that (14) is not analytic. And yet its truth is independent of experience because we accept no single experience as a refutation of it. That is, we may be unable to find the cause of a particular event; this does not lead us to postulate, however, that it was uncaused, but merely that we are ignorant of the cause.

Though it is sometimes asserted that the analytic-synthetic and the *a priori-a posteriori* distinctions are in reality one distinction (and that only groups I and IV are legitimate), such a view requires careful arguments for its support. The distinction between analytic and *a priori* is at least nominally clear and should not be blurred. The criterion for analyticity has to do with logical structure and word meanings, while the criterion for something's being *a priori* is its relation to evidence and experience.

Of course, even when the distinctions are clear and precise, we may have trouble deciding the status of particular sentences. As a final example, consider the following:

(15) All swans are white.

Suppose this assertion is made by a biologist soon after the discovery and naming of the species 'swan', and before black swans have yet been observed. The status of (15) may be in doubt. If it is an *a posteriori* synthetic sentence, then it is only probably true and the appearance of one black swan-like bird will refute it. On the other hand, we may take (15) as *a priori* analytic, expressing one of the necessary properties for a bird's being a swan. Then the black swan-like bird might be denied the title 'swan', and categorized as a member of a different though related species. (Or we might amend the defining characteristics to include black as well as white swans—as we do in fact.)

5. *Some Contemporary Views*

In the two hundred years since Kant wrote about these distinctions, they have never ceased to play a significant role in philosophical inquiry. As we shall indicate in Section 6 below, some of the recurring problems in philosophy, particularly since Descartes, can be formulated directly in terms of the analytic-synthetic, *a priori-a posteriori* distinctions. In view of this, it is not surprising that much work has gone into the attempt to clarify these key concepts and to test the validity of the distinctions.

Some have asserted that there is, in principle, a fundamental imprecision in the concept of synonymy, which is fatal to the analytic-synthetic distinction. It is also asserted by some that the *a priori-a posteriori* distinction stands or falls with the analytic-snythetic distinction, while others hold that the former distinction may be maintained even though the latter should be given up.

Such controversies are not yet settled, and it is not the purpose of this section to explore them further. Rather, these contemporary views have been mentioned to emphasize the fact that the definitions of 'analytic', '*a priori*', etc. given in Sections 2-4 above, are those traditionally given, and are not to be taken as precise or adequate to all the work they are called upon to do. At best, what has been explained above can serve as a starting point for further inquiry, and these distinctions, though rough, can be used to shed some light on some of the perennial philosophical issues.

6. *Empiricism and Rationalism*

The distinctions we have been discussing help to make clear the fundamental difference between empiricism and rationalism. This difference can be set forth quite simply. Rationalists hold that there are *a priori* synthetic sentences, and they typically try to prove that certain basic assertions do have this status. Empiricists, on the other hand, insist that every true sentence is either analytic or else synthetic *a posteriori*.

This dichotomy is especially clear in the case of Hume and Kant. It was largely in an attempt to provide an alternative to Hume's empiricism and the skepticism to which it led him that Kant developed the analytic-synthetic distinction and the concept of *a priori* knowledge. Since the eighteenth century, the formulation of the empiricist-rationalist controversy in terms of that distinction has remained virtually unaltered. (As mentioned in Section 5 above, some doubt has recently been cast on the precision of the analytic-synthetic distinction, and this may lead to a reformulation of the point at issue.)

Further, the views of the rationalists and empiricists who preceded Hume and Kant can also be characterized according to their stand on the existence of *a priori* synthetic knowledge, although, generally, they did not explicitly employ the analytic-synthetic distinction.

The point here is not merely to label opposing sides of a long-standing philosophical controversy, but to indicate the essential difference between these two positions. At the same time, one must be careful not to overlook the significant differences between proponents of a single school. Descartes and Kant were both rationalists, according to the criterion we are using, but there are many important differences between their views.

VII

Definition and Philosophical Analysis

1. Definition and Explication

A major technique of analytic philosophy is to try to formulate precisely the meanings of terms which, for one reason or another, are of special interest. This sort of philosophical activity dates back to the Greeks and their attempts to discover the nature of beauty, knowledge, justice, and goodness. Our present-day efforts to analyze such terms as 'good' and 'right' are the modern counterpart to the ancients' search for the essence of virtue and goodness. Thus, to say to a philosopher, "Define your terms. Tell me what you mean by 'good' and then we can begin to do ethics," is to misunderstand completely the nature of analytic philosophy. For the philosopher who can specify precisely what the meaning of 'good' is has already achieved some of the purposes with which one might set out to do ethics. Yet it is not as if we do not know at all what 'good' means. If that were so, then we would have no basis for objecting when someone told us, for example, that 'good' means the same as 'weighs between 7 and 34 lbs'. We know that this is not what 'good' means, because, as speakers of English, we have an intuitive understanding of the word. But that is not at all the same as being able to provide a precise and well-formulated definition of the term. Rather, we evaluate proposed definitions by comparing them with our intuitive understanding.

The dictionary, of course, provides definitions of all the terms that interest us. But dictionary definitions are not the kind that are of interest to philosophy, first, because dictionaries usually tell how words are used, and secondly because dictionary definitions are circular. Let us now see what these two limitations of dictionary definitions imply. First, remember that we are seeking the meanings of terms. But telling how a word is used does not altogether give its meaning, because the use of a word is not the same as its meaning. Of course, in general, words could not be used the way they are if they didn't have the meanings they have, and they would not have the meanings they have if they were used differently. Use and meaning are thus closely related. But they are not quite the same. Consider the word 'angel'. We may *use* the word to describe an exceptional woman, but we don't intend to suggest that the woman literally *is* an angel. Rather, we are using the word metaphorically, in a way that depends on its literal meaning. We intend to suggest that the woman has certain angel-like qualities. It is just because the word 'angel' *means* what it does, that we can use it to describe something that is not really an angel.

The second limitation of dictionary definitions has to do with their circularity. Suppose, as an aesthetician, I am concerned to discover the nature of aesthetic value. I may begin by seeking the meaning of 'beautiful'. If I am told that 'x is beautiful' means 'x has beauty', I have been given a definition which surely everyone would agree is correct. But it is of no philosophical value, because it defines the word 'beautiful' in terms of the notion of beauty, and that is just what we set out to analyze. The definition has led us right back where we started: it is circular.

Some definitions are circular in a less obvious way. For example, someone might suggest as a definition of 'x is beautiful' the expression 'x enjoys the characteristic of positive aesthetic merit'. The circularity here is not as apparent as in the previous case. But a moment's reflection reveals that the term we are interested in is defined in terms of a concept we do not understand, and, as if that alone were not enough to make the definition unsatisfactory, it was the attempt to understand that very concept that led us to seek the meaning of 'beautiful'. Thus here, too, we are led back to the place where we began; the circle is a bit larger, but it is none the less a circle.

At this point, we should note that the word 'definition' is used ambiguously. That is, if we seek the meaning of A, and we are told that A means the same as B, we may speak of B as the definition of A. But we may also speak of the entire expression 'A means the same as B' as a definition. Since, in doing analytic philosophy, we wish to be as clear and precise as possible, we must find a way to eliminate the possibility of confusion arising from this ambiguity in the word 'definition'. We thus distinguish A and B as follows: We call the term which is defined the *definiendum*. In this case A is the definiendum. The term which gives the meaning of the definiendum—in this case, B—is called the *definiens*. We call the entire expression 'A means the same as B' a definition. Equivalently, we may say that A is equal to B *by definition*, which we abbreviate as:

$A =_{df} B$, writing the definiendum on the left, and definiens on the right.

It is a common opinion among people unfamiliar with analytic philosophy that the solution of philosophical problems is "just a matter of definition." They observe that any conclusion can be made to follow if one is permitted to define terms at will. For example, if I wish to show that causes must precede their effects in time, and I define 'cause' as 'an event which results in a later event', the conclusion I want is guaranteed by the definition. But the crucial point here is that one is *not* free to define terms at will. On the contrary, there are criteria that a definition must meet if it is to be philosophically acceptable. Thus, merely finding a definition that will support the desired conclusion is not enough. The definition must also meet the criteria, and the criteria make tasks that are "just a matter of definition" very difficult, indeed.

We have already seen what some of the criteria for definition are. Definitions must be in accord with intuitive understanding of the definiendum, and they must not be circular. In addition, the definiens must be expressed in language that we understand, or the definition is of no use to us. Besides, if we do not understand the definiens, there may be a hidden circularity in the definition. These criteria, in most philosophically interesting cases, are either very hard or impossible to meet. Consequently, the technique of *explication* has been developed as an alternative to definition.

The primary difference between explication and definition is that the criterion of accord with intuitive understanding is weakened in the former case. Outside of that, explication is much like definition. In fact, by analogy with definition, we introduce the technical terms *explicandum* and *explicatum* to refer respectively to the term we explicate and the term or phrase we provide as a substitute for it. In seeking an explication for a term, we wish to capture as much of the meaning as we can characterize precisely. Thus, while we do insist on accord with intuitive understanding, we permit some deviation, in the interest of gaining precision. For example, if we wish to explicate 'true', we might try as an explicatum the phrase 'in correspondence with the facts', even though this explicatum does not capture the meaning of 'true' as it is used in, say, 'a true Rembrandt' or 'a true woman'.

2. *Further Methods of Analysis*

Finding definitions or explications for philosophically important terms is not, of course, one of the primary goals of philosophy. It is, rather, a technique used in the pursuit of those goals. There are many other techniques that play a prominent part in philosophical analysis. Providing a *counter-example*, for instance, is a simple yet essential technique. A counter-example is merely an example which illustrates that a given general assertion is false. Consider the assertion that no United States President has ever been a Catholic. The fact that John F. Kennedy was both a Catholic and a United States President is a counter-example to that assertion. Or consider the assertion that no state is larger than Texas. The fact that Alaska is a state and is larger than Texas is the counter-example to that assertion. Similarly, if I assert that 'knowledge' $=_{df}$ 'belief'—that is, that 'belief' means the same as 'knowledge'—then the fact that one may be said to believe something, yet not to know it (if, for example, it is false), provides a counter-example to my assertion that 'belief' means the same as 'knowledge'. We call such an illustration a counter-example to the definition.

Another important philosophical technique is that of

reductio ad absurdum. That is, we show a position to be unacceptable by showing that it leads to—or can be reduced to—something absurd or clearly unacceptable for some other reason. For example, consider the assertion that there is no reason for keeping a promise. We apply the technique as follows. We consider what 'There is no reason to keep a promise' means, by considering what a promise is. A promise, by its very nature, is obligatory. If someone makes a promise, then he has an obligation to keep it. Of course, something may happen to override that obligation; that is, there may be strong reasons not to keep the promise. But there is always some reason to keep it, simply because, as a promise, it involves an obligation to do something, and the existence of an obligation to do something is a reason for doing it. The assertion we began with was that there is no reason for keeping a promise. But we have now seen that a promise is by its very nature something which there is a reason to keep. So the assertion comes down to saying that there is no reason to do something which by its very nature there is a reason to do. Since this is absurd, the claim must be rejected —*if* our argument is valid *and* our assumptions about the nature of promises are acceptable.

Finally, let us consider a somewhat more detailed illustration of philosophical analysis. The concept of causation is a prominent subject of philosophical inquiry. Consider the assertion that the same cause can have many effects. If we wish to be in a position to judge whether or not this assertion is true, we must first become clear about what it means. But its meaning is really not clear at all, in spite of the fact that it may at first glance appear to be a simple assertion. In fact, we can distinguish a number of different ways in which it may be taken, and it may turn out that whether we judge the assertion to be true or false depends on which way we take it. This situation is a standard one in analytic philosophy, where we are often faced with the task of evaluating an assertion which is actually ambiguous.

If we wish to understand the assertion in question, we must first achieve some clarity about the terms used. If we have no understanding of the word 'cause', then we cannot understand an assertion about causes. The first thing we note is that the word 'cause' is itself used ambiguously. That is, we sometimes speak of a *particular* event as a cause, as when we say "When you went out without a hat, that (your going out last night without a hat) caused your cold." But sometimes we speak of a *kind* of event as a cause, as when we say "Going out without a hat causes colds." Here we are not speaking of any particular event, but of the entire class of events of a certain kind—the class of events which can be described as instances of going out without a hat. Now we can distinguish particular events (e.g., *your* going out without a hat *last* night) from kinds of events (e.g., going out without a hat). We can give a name to a particular event—let us refer to your going out last night without a hat as 'p'. Thus, we can say "p caused your cold." Let us also give a name to the kind of event in question. We will say that an event is an event of kind A if it is an instance of going out without a hat. Thus, p is an event of kind A. There is just one p; it is a particular event. But there can be any number of events of kind A.

Now we are in a position to see the ambiguity in the claim "The same cause can have many effects." First, we see that the phrase 'the same cause' could refer to a *particular* event. An example might be p—your going out without a hat last night. One might then say that p can have many effects. But the phrase 'the same cause' might refer to causes of the same kind. Thus, if I too go

out without a hat and I get a cough, one might say that
the cause of my cough is the same as the cause of your
cold. That is *not* to say that event p caused my cough.
Rather, it is to say that my cough and your cold were
both caused by events of the same kind, kind A.

We shall now distinguish two senses of the assertion
in question. 'The same cause can have many effects'
may mean:

> (1) Two different events of the same type (e.g.,
>   A) can have effects of different types (e.g.,
>   coughs or colds).
> (2) One event (e.g., p) can have many effects.

But (2) is itself ambiguous, because the phrase 'many
effects' is in need of analysis. For example, if we say
that p can have many effects, we may mean that the
event p can result in a reprimand from your wife when
you return, *and* a cold tomorrow, *and* loss of hair later.
We are saying that one event (p) can have many subsequent effects (say, a, b, and c). On the other hand,
we might mean that there are several different possible
events any one of which could result from p, depending on the circumstances. For example, p could result
in your getting a cold if it rains, *or* your winning a bet
(e.g., that if you leave your hat at home it will not
rain) if it doesn't. Thus, we are saying that one event
(p) can result in one of many effects (b or d or e),
depending on what happens. Thus (2) may mean:

> (2a) One event (e.g., p) can have many subse-
>   quent effects, or
> (2b) One event (e.g., p) can have various out-
>   comes, depending on the circumstances.

We shall not carry the analysis any further, nor shall
we be concerned with evaluating assertions (1), (2a),

and (2b). Rather, we intend the analysis carried out so far to provide an illustration of actual philosophical activity, and an example of the care with which such activity must be performed.

VIII

Reading and Writing Philosophy

1. Reading Philosophy

The fact that philosophical writing is typically discursive, and sometimes of great literary merit, must not mislead one into thinking that philosophy books can be digested rapidly or understood on first reading. Indeed, the student is well advised to approach a philosophy book much as he would approach a physics text or an essay in mathematics.

It is impossible, of course, to lay down a set of rules about how one must read philosophy. Every person should develop his own method of reading and understanding written material. Therefore, the following remarks should be regarded as a suggested approach to the reading of philosophy, setting forth what will generally be found to be the minimum requirements for understanding a piece of philosophical discourse.

A. Read the work through to the end, sympathetically, in order to become familiar with the organization of the book, the author's style and the major problems to which the book is addressed.

B. Reread the book more carefully; try to isolate the issues and arguments.

C. Read the book in detail, proceeding slowly and analyzing each argument as it arises. One may want to outline certain passages or translate particular arguments into the notation of symbolic logic in order to clarify their structure.

D. Reread the book *in toto,* to grasp the overall aims and conclusions of the author and to evaluate the consistency of his argument. It is only at this point, after each component argument has been mastered, that the work can be completely understood.

Philosophy, like most technical writing, must be read *actively.* One must carry on a silent dialogue with the author, questioning him at every turn and accepting his conclusions only after they have been carefully tested. The following are some questions that should be kept in mind while reading, particularly when one is analyzing the arguments in detail (step C, above).

What problem is the author trying to solve? Does his formulation of the problem rest on any assumptions, tacit or explicitly stated?

How is he treating the problem? What is his method of solution?

On what assumptions does the author base his arguments?

What assumptions are needed for his argument, even though not explicitly stated by him?

Is his argument valid? Is it sound?

How does each particular argument fit into the work as a whole? Is it necessary to the main argument?

If the author has made a mistake, is it an instructive one? How is it that he was led astray? Perhaps in formulating an answer to this last question, we will hit upon a general mistake, which is likely to be made in other contexts as well.

2. Writing Philosophy

Analytic philosophy is an activity that is pursued in the hope of achieving precision and clarity about the concepts, logical structure, methods and objects of human knowledge. Thus, precision and clarity are minimal criteria of acceptability in philosophical writing. But precision and clarity, sad to say, are as hard to achieve as excellence in style. Whoever wishes to do philosophical analysis, therefore, must consciously endeavor to meet the standards that the discipline imposes.

As with other kinds of writing, the only way to learn to write philosophy is by making the attempt. One must write, subject the result to careful criticism, and then write again, bearing in mind the criticism. But it is not only others who can provide such beneficial criticism. On the contrary, the ability to read one's own writing with critical scrutiny is a major asset to writers of all sorts, and a mark of successful writers in any field. Yet one can be usefully critical, of oneself or of others, only to the extent to which one has standards of criticism.

Everything that has been said above about reading philosophy is equally true when it is one's own philosophy that is being read. Thus, remarks about what to look for when reading philosophy provide some basis for self-criticism in writing philosophy. If one knows what to look for in the writing of others, then one can, insofar as it is possible to remain objective, evaluate one's own work. But the tendency is to read one's own writing with extraordinary sympathy—to overlook failings which would be immediately apparent in the writing of others. Thus, reading one's own philosophy critically is generally more difficult than reading the work of others.

Some progress in the effort to be objectively self-critical may result from explicit consideration of the nature of common failings in philosophical writing. Such consideration should, at least, alert the beginning writer of philosophy to specific dangers to which he is likely to fall victim. We shall, therefore, present in the remainder of this section a discussion of some characteristic weaknesses of beginning papers in philosophy. The material in the following two sections should be of some use in helping the writer to avoid those weaknesses.

Beginning writing in philosophy is commonly very unclear. This lack of clarity results from many factors, some of which can be explicitly isolated. Among the most common are:

A. The use of phrases and expressions which have no meaning, or no meaning that is clear in the context. Consider in this connection the phrase 'the *nearly infinite* value of a human life'. What does 'nearly infinite' mean—large but finite? Or actually infinite?

B. The use of equivocal terms or phrases (i.e. ambiguous terms or phrases) as if they were univocal. Consider: 'The *purpose* of this knife is to cut grapefruit'. Does 'purpose' in this sentence mean the purpose for which the knife was designed or the purpose for which it is used? It might be a knife designed specifically to cut grapefruit, or it might be a bent steak knife that is used to cut grapefruit.

C. Reliance on unexplained metaphors or analogies. For example, 'The human mind is like a computer'. In what specific ways is it like a computer? Not in being made of metal.

D. Reliance on jargon—that is, the use of phrases

which have a familiar or authoritative ring, but little content. Consider: 'Without absolute standards there can be no moral worth'. The phrase 'absolute standard' is a familiar one, but it is used in so many different ways that its meaning in this context is not clear.

More generally, papers in philosophy commonly suffer from a lack of substantial content. This lack is often due in part to one or more of the following mistakes:

A. Failure to take note of important relevant distinctions, e.g. failing to distinguish, in a paper about values, between what *is* and what *ought to be*.

B. Overemphasis of a single aspect of a problem— e.g. in a discussion of principles of education, speaking of man as an economic or intellectual being, without mentioning or justifying the restriction to these aspects of man.

C. Failure to formulate the problem at hand in a precise and clear way.

D. Failure to come to grips with a problem once it is formulated. This failing frequently results in papers which, while not containing assertions or arguments that are themselves objectionable, provide more wind than substance. Usually, assertions in papers of this type, if they are intelligible, are so vague and general that it is difficult to imagine how they could be doubted, or why they need be said.

E. Failure to perceive the lack of precision in ordinary language. Just what, for example, does it mean to say, as people often do, that morality is objective? Is it objective like the weight of a stone—measurable by scientific observation—or what?

F. Failure to reread critically, to insure both that one has said what he has meant to say, and that one means what he has in fact said.

3. Use and Mention

In this section, as throughout this book, we have oc-
casion to talk *about* words, to *mention* a word rather
than to *use* it. The device of using single quotation
marks to indicate that a word is being mentioned and
not used is found frequently in philosophical writings
and is deserving of attention here.

An author writing about Franklin Delano Roosevelt
will have many occasions to mention the thirty-second
President. He will mention Roosevelt, for example, in
any sentence which is about Roosevelt, and he will
mention the thirty-second President by using his name
or some description which uniquely describes Roosevelt. In the preceding two sentences, Roosevelt has
been mentioned six times, four times by using his name
and twice by using a definite description, i.e. 'the thirty-
second President'. A man and his name are quite
different entities; one is an animal, the other an ele-
ment of language. Sentences are composed of elements
of a language; one could not use Roosevelt himself in a
sentence any more than one could shake hands with
Roosevelt's name.

Analogously, when one talks about a word or men-
tions a word in a sentence, one does so by using the
name of that word in the sentence. But the name of a
word is also a word; both are elements of language,
both can be used in sentences, and thus they may easily be confused. The name of a word is formed by enclosing the word within *single* quotation marks. A
name formed in this way refers to the *word* of which it
is a name, just as Roosevelt's name refers to the man of
whom it is a name. The name of a word does not refer
to the object or objects referred to by the word of
which it is a name. A word may not refer to any object,

but its name always refers to the word, e.g., 'is' does not refer to any object, but ' 'is' ' refers to a word. Let us consider some further examples.

(1) Red is a color.
(2) 'Red' is a three-letter word.
(3) John is a boy.
(4) 'John' is a boy's name.

Each of these sentences is true, while the following sentences are false.

(5) Red is a three-letter word.
(6) 'Red' is a color.
(7) 'John' is a boy.
(8) John is a boy's name.

Sentence (5) is false because it states that a color is a word, while (6) is false because it states that a word is a color. (7) and (8) reveal a similar confusion of a name with the name of a name. Sometimes we may wish to refer to a word in a sentence; consider these examples:

(9) 'Red' in sentence (5) refers to a color.
(10) ' 'Red' ' in sentence (6) refers to a word.
(11) ' 'Red' ' appears in sentence (6), but 'red' does not.

Each of these sentences is true, but the following sentence is false because it states that a word which refers to a color refers to a word:

(12) 'Red' in sentence (5) refers to a word.

We may form the name of a sentence, a predicate or a description in an analogous way. Consider:

(13) 'John believes it hailed yesterday' is an intensional sentence.

> (14) 'is a Senator from California' is a predicate of Senator Kuchel.
>
> (15) 'The Senator from California' fails to describe one and only one individual.

Notice that the following sentence is not even grammatically correct, because there is no subject of the verb 'is'.

> (16) John believes it hailed yesterday is an intensional sentence.

In sentence (10) we used the name of a name of a word. We form the name of a name just as we form the name of any other word, by enclosing the name in single quotation marks. Similarly we can form the name of a name of a name, etc., the limit to this procedure being one of intelligibility rather than one of logic.

4. Words to Watch

Words are used for various purposes. Some words that suffice for everyday communication do not suffice for philosophical discussions, perhaps because they are vague in their ordinary use. Or perhaps it is because it has been to the philosopher's interest to draw fine distinctions with which one is not concerned outside of philosophical study and which therefore are not reflected in words as they are ordinarily used. Below we shall mention some words and phrases that are best avoided in philosophical discussions and some that should be used only with considered caution.

Semantics is most commonly understood by philosophers as theory of meaning, encompassing questions about the sense and reference of words. As such, it is concerned with the relations between a sign (or word) and what the sign signifies (or means). Semantics in this sense may be contrasted with syntactics, which is concerned in part with formal relations between signs, and with the rules by which signs may be combined to yield well-formed formulas (sentences) in a given language. There are indeed many *semantical questions*, including those problems concerning sentences, words and meaning mentioned above in Chapters IV and V, as well as questions in the theory of truth, and questions concerning the relations between a name and the object it names. But to say that something is "just a matter of semantics" or "just a question of semantics" can be misleading. We have seen in the previous discussion of philosophical analysis that definitions in accord with strict criteria may be a goal of some philosophical investigation. But to suppose that one can dismiss a philosophical problem by asserting that "it is just a matter of definition or semantics" is to miss the point of what a philosophical problem is, if such an assertion is intended to imply that the problem can be solved by arbitrarily defining certain terms. Arbitrary definitions will not solve any philosophical problem.

Whether it is sentences or propositions that can be true, a particular sentence or proposition is either true or false. To say that a sentence is *really true* is to say no more than that it is true. And to say that one sentence is *more true* or *closer to the truth* than another is often to engender confusion. If two sentences are both true, they are equally true. If both are false, then neither is true, nor is one more true than the other. If one sentence is true and another false, it may be appropriate to speak of the first as more true than the second, but this locution does not convey as much information about the sentences as is conveyed simply by saying that one is true and the other false. It may, of course, be that there is better evidence for one sentence than another, or better reason to believe one than another. Instead of referring to one sentence as more true than another, it is clearer to show that the evidence for one is better than that for the other.

The words '*subjective*', '*objective*', '*relative*' and '*absolute*' have often been used by philosophers. But no one of these terms has had only one use. It is safe to say that these words should be avoided as much as possible. Whenever something is said to be relative, one must also say to *what* it is relative. 'What is right is relative' is not a complete assertion until one has said whether what is right is relative to a particular society, or individual, or whatever. When 'absolute' is used with the intention of conveying the idea 'not relative', the question 'not relative to what' becomes relevant. Like 'relative' and 'absolute', the words 'subjective' and 'objective' have often been assumed to be opposite in meaning. But since none of these four words has either a clear meaning or a standardized use in philosophical discussions, this opposition is of no help in clarifying the meaning of any of these words. It is worth noting that 'subjective' need not be a pejorative adjective, nor 'objective' an adjective of commendation. Each of these words should be used only with an explanation of how and why it is being used. Often such an explanation suffices to make the point for which the word seemed useful.

The words discussed below are used clearly only when certain questions are answered about each particular use. Consider the assertion that two events or objects are *similar, alike,* or *different.* Such assertions are interesting only when it is said in what respects the things are similar or different, because no matter how different any two things are, there is some respect in which they are alike, and no matter how similar or alike two things are, they are different in some respect. For example, two sentences may be alike in both being extensional, but different in their truth value; two objects may be without perceptible difference in color, size, and shape, and yet be in different places. Referring back to Section 1 of Chapter III, you will see that analogous remarks are applicable to the word 'same'. We often say of one object that it is different from what it once was, that it has *changed* or is *changing*. Just as one needs to specify in what ways two different things are different, so must one say in what respects one and the same thing has changed or is different. The assertion that two objects or events are the same and yet different need not be contradictory, although it may be. Its meaning simply is not clear until it is indicated in what respect, or in relation to which properties, the objects are the same and different.

The words *'efficient'*, *'deficient'*, *'perfect'*, *'complete'* and *'adequate'* similarly call for an answer to the questions "In what respects?" or "By what standards?" or "For what purposes?" Thus a knife may be efficient for cutting meat and inefficient for turning screws. A rose may be a perfect flower, but an imperfect source of nourishment. A student's program of study may be adequate for a high school diploma, but inadequate for college admission. And a cereal may be complete as a supply of vitamin requirements for a child, but incomplete for an adolescent.

The words *'object'*, *'entity'*, and *'thing'* must be used with one caution in mind. None of these words provides a criterion for individuation; that is, one can know the meaning of the word 'thing' and still be unable to distinguish one thing from another. In contrast, if one knows the meaning of the word 'man', he can distinguish one man from another, or count the number of men in a room. But suppose that one were asked to count the number of things or objects in a room in which there were ten men. He would not know whether to count each man's leg as an entity; he would not know whether to count men's arms as well as men's hands as things. Thus to say of anything that it is an entity or an object or a thing is to provide little or no information about it.

Words or sentences that have no clearly defined meaning or use may be said to be *vague*. The word 'absolute' is vague, as is the sentence 'There are no absolute standards of morality'. In contrast, an *ambiguous* word or sentence is one which has more than one meaning. 'Bridge' is an ambiguous word, and if Jones is a man who builds spans over water and wears false teeth, the sentence 'Jones's new bridge is poorly designed' is ambiguous. It is also said that a word or sentence is *meaningless*. Some philosophers have asserted that the sentence 'God exists' is meaningless because it is neither analytic nor confirmable by experience. Clearly such an assertion presupposes a standard of meaningfulness—namely, that any statement which is meaningful is either analytic or subject to empirical confirmation. So when a word or sentence is asserted to be meaningless, the question "By what criterion of meaningfulness?" is in order. Most frequently, the assertion that a sentence is meaningless is intended to indicate that the sentence has no content and conveys no information. Therefore, a meaningless sentence is neither true nor false; that is, it has no content on the basis of which its truth value could be determined.

IX

Divisions of Philosophy

1. *Introduction*

Philosophy is a broad field of study within which it is
possible to delimit more specific areas of inquiry. Such
divisions have been made traditionally on the basis of
the nature of the questions considered in each area. In
this chapter, we shall deal with the general content of
the major areas of philosophy by indicating some problems illustrative of each area. But these problems we
mention will hardly be exhaustive of the areas; rather,
they are selected as typical. Moreover, it is a serious
error to suppose that a question in philosophy falls
neatly within one specialized area. In fact, there are
many problems in philosophy that are of major concern to specialists in several areas. In such cases, one
can think of the areas in philosophy as representing not
so much various sets of questions, but rather various
points of view from which the questions are to be considered. Thus, it is rare indeed that real progress in one
area of philosophy does not shed some light in other
areas. And as one might expect, a mark of the importance of a problem in philosophy is the extent to which

it permeates the various divisions within the field. The picture we will provide of the divisions of philosophy will thus be rough—but that is well, for the divisions are rough, and it would be a great mistake to consider them to be clearly delineated.

2. *Theory of Value*

A. ETHICS

We evaluate our own and others' actions; for example:

> (1) Dr. Smith will do the *right* thing if he tells his patient the truth about his illness.
>
> (2) I am *obligated* to repay the money I borrowed from Bill.

Evaluations can also be made of kinds of actions; for example:

> (3) It is always *right* to tell the truth.
>
> (4) Repaying debts is *obligatory*.

And evaluations can be made of people as agents, i.e. persons who act; for example:

> (5) Smith did not have to accept the offer; he was *free* to do as he chose.
>
> (6) Jones was *worthy of praise* for saving Brown from drowning.

Speaking generally, we might say that each of these examples is an assertion about moral value. Ethics is, in part, an investigation into the nature of moral judgment and moral reasoning. Typical of the questions which fall within the scope of ethics is the following: If a man says that an act is right, is he just saying something about himself—for example, that he approves of the act; or is he saying something about a property,

rightness, which the act has independently of his attitude? Closely linked with this question is the question
of what facts about the act one could cite as evidence
for the correctness of judgments of the kinds exemplified above by (1) to (6). If such a judgment is only a
report of the feelings of the judge toward the act, is
any evidence relevant to determining the truth value of
the judgment?

Questions in ethics then are not questions about
whether a particular act is right or wrong; ethics is to
be distinguished from moralizing or casuistry. Ethical
arguments are not exhortations to some course of action. It is true that philosophers writing in ethics have
not always avoided giving moral advice. But ethical
philosophers, *qua* philosophers, discuss instead the *nature of reasoning* about moral matters, and propose criteria on the basis of which such reasoning is to be eval-
uated.

What distinguishes good from bad reasons offered in
favor of moral judgments? One sometimes supports a
particular judgment (for example, 1 above) by appeal
to a general principle (for example, 3 above). But philosophers have been concerned to determine in just
what way general principles do support particular
claims. Imagine a disagreement between Mr. Black
and Mr. White. Black argues that (1) is a correct judgment because the doctor's telling his patient the truth
is a particular instance of the kind of action mentioned
in (3). White denies that (1) is correct; he cites another general principle, that a doctor is obliged to do
whatever is possible to improve his patient's condition.
White asserts that this patient's condition would be
worsened by his knowledge of the severity of his condition, and therefore that for Dr. Smith to tell the patient the truth must be wrong because to do so is to

violate the doctor's obligation to improve his patient's health.

This supposed disagreement raises several problems which have concerned ethical philosophers. First we see that the general principles to which White and Black appeal support conflicting judgments about the moral value of a particular act. Perhaps we must evaluate the general principles before we can judge the cogency of the arguments presented. One might ask whether there can be evidence for general principles at all; perhaps we should evaluate a principle by inquiring into the acceptability of the particular judgments it supports. But if we argue that general principles support particular judgments, and that acceptability of a general principle is to be decided on the basis of the judgments it supports, our argument seems to be circular.

In this dispute, White cited a fact about the patient's condition, the fact that the patient's condition would be worsened if he learned of the severity of his illness. Philosophers have often discussed the role that facts such as this, which do not themselves involve value judgments, play in moral reasoning. Is it always possible to distinguish descriptive or factual claims from evaluative claims? How can factual evidence ever be relevant to moral judgments?

It has often been argued that unless one understands the meaning of such terms as 'right', 'obligatory', 'free', and 'responsible', which are used in ethical judgments, one cannot begin to answer other questions in ethics. Thus some writers in ethics have attempted to define 'right' or the rightness of an action, either in terms of its consequences, or in terms of the motives from which it was done. Other writers have argued that no non-circular definition is possible. Still others have argued that such terms as 'right' have no meaning, but rather are used simply to express approval.

Inquiry into the meaning of expressions used in ethical judgments is relevant to the question of what is evidence for a moral judgment. If we believe that 'right' means 'done from altruistic motives', then whatever is evidence that an act was done from altruistic motives is at the same time evidence that the act was right. The question of evidence is central to the problem of evaluating a person's moral reasoning or of adjudicating between the disputants in an argument concerning matters of value.

Discussion of the rightness or wrongness of actions has been closely connected with discussions of the moral worth of agents. Philosophers have been concerned to discuss what reasons are relevant to the evaluation of a person as, for example, praiseworthy or blameworthy for an action. Problems concerning the logical relations between a person's being free and his being responsible, and between his being responsible and his being worthy of praise or blame, have been considered throughout the history of ethical philosophy.

B. AESTHETICS

Not all evaluations are of actions; not all value is ethical value. We judge one painting to be better than another, evaluate the rhythm of a poem, criticize the form of a sculpture. One studies such evaluations in aesthetics, but judgments about beauty are not limited to works of art. They may apply as well to natural objects and events, such as mountains and sunsets. Thus, aesthetics is not limited to the study of evaluations of artifacts. In fact, one of the questions that interests aestheticians is whether or not there is any way to delimit the range of objects that can have aesthetic value.

Analogously to questioning in ethics, one might ask whether or not the beauty of an object can be defined in terms of some or all of the object's descriptive properties or qualities. Does the subject matter of a work of art contribute to its aesthetic value? For example, if kindness is better than cruelty, is a poem praising kindness better than one praising cruelty?

The question also arises whether there can be any basis for criticizing someone's judgment that a painting or poem is beautiful. Is such a judgment merely an expression of taste? Or do aesthetic judgments, like those in science, stand in need of justification? If so, how can they be defended?

Aesthetics is not art criticism; aestheticians are not concerned to evaluate particular works of art or to advise artists how to create better works of art. Rather, aestheticians have typically been concerned with such questions as whether there is an aesthetic attitude, a particular way in which one must regard an object, in order to appreicate its aesthetic value or beauty. Writers in aesthetics have proposed and criticized criteria for the evaluation of aesthetic judgments; they have proposed and criticized general principles which might support particular judgments; finally, they have often discussed whether any such criteria are even possible.

3. *Epistemology*

There are many things which we claim to know—for example: (1) that all men are animals, (2) that Lassie is a collie, (3) that cigarette smoking is causally related to lung cancer, and (4) that every event has a cause. We are not usually called upon to justify our claims to knowledge. But if someone were to assert that there were green men living on Mars, we might well ask him how he knew or what his evidence was. If he replied that he knew because he had seen green Martians in his crystal ball, we would question both the acceptability of his evidence and the truth of his original assertion.

Epistemology is an inquiry into the nature of knowledge. But the epistemologist is not asking what the evidence is for *particular* knowledge claims. Rather, part of the inquiry of epistemology is directed toward ascertaining what *kind* of evidence is relevant to a particular *kind* of knowledge claim. It was the observation that there are different kinds of claims to knowledge, requiring different sorts of evidence, which led philosophers to draw the distinctions discussed above (Chapter VI) between analytic and synthetic sentences and between *a priori* and *a posteriori* knowledge.

In the course of investigating the relation between the evidence for an assertion and the assertion itself, the epistemologist may ask whether the evidence must be known with certainty. For example, does the fact that we may sometimes be deceived by our senses invalidate perception as a source of evidence? Since the evidence for some claims [such as (2) above] must be at least in part perceptual, if one argues that perception is not a reliable source of evidence, he thereby argues that no empirical statement like (2) can ever be known to be true. And, in so arguing, he would be offering a partial answer to one epistemological question—what sorts of things can we know?

We have suggested that the task of the epistemologist differs from that of the scientist. Consider, as illustrative of the point, the question of how we are able to see colors. The physicist or physiologist may take this question to be equivalent to the question of how we make color discriminations. He may then study physical conditions of sight such as illumination, eye structure, and neurological connections between the eye and the brain. The philosopher, on the other hand, may argue that we do not see colors at all. What we see, he may claim, are colored objects. If A sees X, then X appears some way to A. But colors don't appear any way to anyone. Objects can appear red, but how does red appear? Does it ever look orange? Objects can appear different than they are, but how can colors do this? Thus, the philosopher's approach is that of conceptual analysis of what it means to say that someone sees something.

Another problem typical of epistemological inquiry concerns the status of induction as a source of evidence for claims to knowledge.

Inductive arguments begin with particular observation statements or a statement summarizing particular observations; they have as conclusions either (1) a general statement, not all of whose particular instances are known, or (2) a particular statement about an as yet unknown state of affairs. An example of (1) is:

> All Presidents of the United States thus far have
> been men.
> (Therefore) All Presidents of the United States
> will be men.

And an example of (2) is:

> All Presidents of the United States thus far have
> been men.
> (Therefore) The next President of the United
> States will be a man.

Neither of these arguments is deductively valid; it is logically possible that the next President of the United States will be a woman, even though the above premise is true.

Although logicians have criteria for the admissibility of rules of deductive inference, as well as a complete and sound set of rules which satisfy these criteria, no such criteria or set of rules exist for inductive arguments. And because it is always logically possible that the conclusion of an inductive argument may be false even though its premises are true, some philosophers have argued that induction does not provide an acceptable source of evidence, that the mere fact that some proposition is the conclusion of an inductive argument cannot constitute sufficient reason for a claim to know that that proposition is true. The philosophical discussion of induction resembles the discussion of the status of perceptual evidence in that it is a general inquiry into what, if anything, constitutes good evidence for a particular type of claim.

Argument by analogy is sometimes considered a type of inductive argument. Attention has been directed toward the question of the validity of this kind of argument because it has seemed a method by which we might justify claims of knowledge about others' minds—for example, about what another person believes. We cannot observe another's mind, but we can observe his actions. Suppose Mr. Smith is acting exactly as I do when I believe that it is going to rain today. When I act as he is now acting, I do so because I believe it will rain today. I can observe these likenesses in behavior, and then conclude that we are alike in beliefs as well, i.e. that he believes it is going to rain today. Yet there is always the logical possibility that he acts as he does because he holds a belief different from mine, e.g. that taking an umbrella will prevent rain. In an argument by analogy, it is observed that some things have certain of their properties the same, in this case that Smith is acting as I act when I believe it will rain. On the basis of the observed similarities, it is concluded that the things are also alike in some unobserved respects, in this case that we are alike in our belief that it will rain.

Not all epistemological questions are directly concerned with the relation between evidence and a proposition which someone claims to know. We claim to know not only propositions but how to do things—how to swim, spell, or play chess. And we claim to know people and places, to know Chief Justice Warren or San Francisco. Philosophers have discussed whether there is any common factor present in all cases of knowing—perhaps a state of mind or the ability to perform in a certain way. The question of what counts as evidence when one claims to know how to swim or to know San Francisco has also been discussed, along with the question of the relation between evidence for these claims and evidence for the truth of propositions.

4. Metaphysics

We have said that many questions are studied from the standpoint of one or another specialized area of philosophy, and that it is impossible to give more than a rough delineation of the divisions within philosophy. Nowhere is it more difficult to isolate an area by reference to its problems than in metaphysics. One reason for this difficulty is that, throughout the history of philosophy, many problems have at one time been called metaphysical and at other times been denied that appellation. Some philosophers, distressed by the sort of speculation which has been called metaphysics, have denied that the problems with which they were concerned were metaphysical ones. Others have argued that these philosophers were nevertheless still dealing with traditional problems of metaphysics, and that no renaming of a problem would change its nature. With

these difficulties in mind, let us make some general remarks about some problems which have most usually
been called metaphysical, and about the status of the
propositions of metaphysics.

Metaphysics is concerned with the way in which we
think about the world. Some metaphysicians have held
that the concepts basic to our thought could not be
other than they are. They have gone on to inquire into
which concepts are necessarily presupposed by the
structure of our thought. We distinguish individuals—
the sorts of things that possess properties, from the
properties they possess. This distinction, often referred
to as that between particulars and universals, has been
cited as an example of a distinction fundamental to our
way of thinking, and it has brought forth many questions in metaphysics. For example, what are the criteria by which we individuate particulars, i.e. distinguish
one particular object from another? On what grounds
do we say that the butterfly which emerges from a cocoon is one and the same animal as the caterpillar that
spun the cocoon? Do the criteria for individuating
people imply that there are some essential properties
which an object must possess in order to be a person?
Suppose, for example, that a person loses all reasoning
power; is what remains still a person? Or are there
some changes a person could undergo, after which
what remains would no longer be a person?

Regarding universals, it has been long debated
whether or not they exist independently of their being
manifested in particulars. Could there, for example, be
whiteness if there were no white objects? Further, one
may ask how universals can be individuated one from
another. Can one explain the difference between redness and greenness with no reference to red or green
particulars?

Not all metaphysicians have accepted the way in

which we normally think about the world as inevitable or even correct. Some have suggested that we alter the structure of our thought, arguing, for example, that the world we perceive through our senses is but an appearance of some transcendent reality. Many have gone on to consider the nature of this supposed reality, suggesting that it consists of some sort of mind or collection of ideas, rather than of physical matter.

Such questions, about just what it is that actually exists, are called *ontological* questions. Thus the question of whether universals exist independently of the particulars which instantiate them is an ontological question. Some philosophers have argued that universals do exist, but in a different sense of the word 'exist' from that in which particulars are said to exist. Whether the word 'exist' is genuinely equivocal in such a way is open to question.

The question of just what kinds of things exist is one of importance to many areas of philosophy, and thus philosophers have studied in detail the consequences of various answers. If matter is held to be the only kind of thing that exists, and if in addition matter is subject to causal laws, can there be freedom of the will? The answer to this question is of importance, for example, in moral and legal philosophy, where questions of responsibility arise. On the other hand, if one is an idealist, i.e. if one holds that ideas alone exist, various epistemological questions arise at once. For instance, how can sensory experience be evidence for a proposition about ideas?

It is often difficult to know what would count as evidence for a metaphysical claim. The proposition that universals exist independently of particulars would usually be regarded as synthetic. Yet it seems totally unsusceptible of an *a posteriori* proof. In general, metaphysical claims are synthetic, but admit only of an *a priori* proof. As you have read in Chapter VI, many philosophers deny that there can be any *a priori* proof of a synthetic statement. Therefore, they question whether metaphysical statements can ever be known to be true. In discussions of the status of metaphysical propositions and the knowledge we can have of them, the distinction between metaphysics and epistemology is difficult, if not impossible, to draw. Similarly, questions of freedom and determinism bring ethics and metaphysics together, and there is a close connection between logic and metaphysics. For in the discussion of the predicate calculus, it was pointed out that the logician must specify the range of his variables, the types of entities for which the variables stand. But what types of entities there are, i.e. what types of things the variables can stand for, is surely a metaphysical question.

5. Logic

Logic is a philosophical study of certain properties of human reasoning. A psychologist might be interested in how people reason: common forms of incorrect reasoning would be as interesting to him as common forms of correct reasoning. But the logician's concern is with an analysis of the structure of correct reasoning. The rules of inference in a system of logic are based on principles of human reasoning, but with the condition that these rules preserve validity—that is, that from true premises they allow the inference only of a true conclusion.

It was pointed out in Chapter I that the validity of an argument depends only on its form. Systems of symbolic logic, with a specified vocabulary and precise rules for forming sentences and drawing inferences, are designed to make the form of an argument as immediately evident as possible. We may regard a system of symbolic logic as a language, an artificial language developed to avoid whenever possible the vagueness and ambiguity inherent in a natural language, such as English or French. When a sentence is translated from English into symbolic notation, it often loses some of the nuances it had in English but, in return for this loss, its logical form is made clear and precise. The relations between a formal and a natural language provide questions which concern the logician as well as the philosopher of language. For example, in a symbolization, just how much of the meaning of a sentence may be sacrificed in the name of precision?

Logicians are also concerned with discovering what properties a system of symbolic logic possesses—e.g., whether it is deductively complete and sound. To say that such a system is complete is to say that *all* the deductions which are valid are allowed by the rules of the system. To say the system is sound is to say that *only* deductively valid inferences are allowed by the rules.

For further insight into the study of logic, the reader should refer to Chapters I and II, and should also see section 6 (below) on philosophy of mathematics.

6. Philosophy of Mathematics

Like philosophers of science and of history, philosophers of mathematics have been concerned with both the methods and the subject matter of the discipline which they study. Most people achieve some proficiency in elementary mathematics without ever questioning the nature of numbers themselves. The philosopher of mathematics considers such questions, asking whether numbers are objects, concepts, properties of sets of objects, or perhaps sets. Further, the philosopher asks what sort of evidence, if any, is relevant to mathematical assertions. A child may make his first acquaintance with numbers by being shown one orange, then two, then three. But this does not show that arithmetical truths are empirical. Rather, one can argue that mathematical propositions are analytic, since it seems that they can be proven by logical and set-theoretical considerations alone. But if we argue that mathematical propositions are analytic, and hence have no extralogical content, we are then faced with the problem of accounting for the apparent relevance of mathematics to the empirical world.

On the other hand, if we hold that mathematical truths are synthetic, we must account for their apparent necessity—for the apparent incoherence inherent in the denial of a truth of mathematics.

Philosophers of mathematics have inquired into the notion of a set, investigating the consistency of intuitive set theory, and seeking to determine whether set theory can be reduced to logic. The relation between numbers and sets is also a matter for investigation. Is it possible, for example, to define numbers in terms of sets? If so, what is to be gained by so doing?

Some of these questions lead us to ask just what would constitute good reasons for believing that mathematical propositions are in fact analytic or synthetic. Such a question has to do with what constitutes a proof *about* mathematics. But we can also ask what constitutes a proof *within* mathematics. And the question of what constitutes such a proof is as much a question of logic as of philosophy of mathematics. Thus, for this among other reasons, the philosophy of mathematics is inseparable from the study of formal logic.

7. Philosophy of Science

There are many notions used in science which the scientist, in his capacity as a scientist, does not usually analyze. There are many presuppositions which he cannot be expected either to make explicit or to justify. (See page 32 regarding the notion of a presupposition.) Nor does the scientist typically investigate the nature of scientific method, of a scientific theory, or of scientific knowledge and the propositions of science. The philosopher of science, however, may be expected to undertake just such tasks as these.

It is obvious that a great deal of material is common to epistemology and the philosophy of science. Among the scientist's presuppositions must surely be some belief in the possibility of empirical knowledge. And any discussion of the nature of a scientific theory will include the question of confirmation, and the notions of induction and probability.

Currently, much discussion in the philosophy of science centers around the problems of explanation and prediction. In order for one to be able to explain a particular phenomenon, must a statement of its occurrence be capable of being deduced from causal laws and from some statements about causal conditions? Is an explanation of this deductive form typical of scientific explanations? Is there only one logical form for an acceptable explanation? What lies behind our conviction that it is a better explanation of a baby's having blue eyes that his parents have blue eyes than that his mother ate blueberries during her pregnancy? Or, in general, why is science preferable to augury? Similar questions may be asked about predictions. What must be the logical form of a prediction if it is to be justified? And what is the relation between the form of an explanation and that of a prediction?

Questions about explanation and prediction are among the many which give rise to questions about causality. What does it mean when a doctor says that an antibiotic injection can have many different effects? An introduction to the kind of interest a philosopher might have in this question is presented in Chapter IV above. Philosophers have been interested in what it means to say that a particular event A caused another event B. Does such an assertion imply that there is a general law about events like A causing events like B? Questions like this present a natural introduction to an inquiry into the nature of scientific laws. One might ask why some general statements are laws, for example, Mendel's laws of genetics, while other true general statements are not, for example, "All children's shoes purchased in California in 1962 cost more than $.05 per pair when new."

What is the justification for theories that bear no obvious relation to everyday experience, and for the introduction of such terms as 'atom', 'proton', 'neutron', and 'electron'? What is the relation between theories involving concepts such as these and the experimental results which these theories purport to explain? And what, if any, are the implications of such theories for philosophical inquiry generally? For example, philosophers have often discussed the concept of time, and have used and discussed the notion of simultaneity. What relevance has Einstein's theory of time to such a discussion? Or again, Heisenberg's uncertainty principle states that in some respects the future cannot be predicted even on the basis of the best possible information about the past and present. Is this principle revelant to the philosopher's discussion of determinism and free will? Or is the will that philosophers have discussed something quite independent of protons, neutrons, and the like? In general we may say that it has been a philosophical question whether science and philosophy constitute different methods of studying the same subject matter or whether the subject matters of the two fields are quite independent of each other.

It has often been assumed that factual claims are more easily verified than value claims, that only factual claims have a place in science, and that the factual results of an experiment are brought into question if they depend on value judgments. Philosophers of science have questioned these assumptions; they have asked whether a scientist, in his role as scientist, makes value judgments, and if so, what effects these judgments have on the status of his experimental results. Is the scientist making a value judgment when he takes something to be a crucial experiment, when he decides that the results of one experiment are to be considered while those of another are to be discarded? If there is any one method which is *the* scientific method, is there any place in such a method for value judgments?

8. *Philosophy of Language*

We use language to communicate with one another; our being able to do so seems to presuppose that at least some of the words in our language have meanings which we understand, and that our understanding is quite similar. But just what is the meaning of a word? And how does a word come to have the meaning it has? These are two general questions with which the philosophy of language is concerned.

In discussing ethics, we noted that it was not concerned with evaluating particular acts and, similarly, that epistemology was not concerned with compiling evidence for particular claims. An analogous disclaimer is in order for philosophy of language: in general, it is not the task of a philosopher investigating language to discover the meanings of particular words, but rather to inquire into the relations among a word, its sense, its reference and the language in which it is a word. In the course of this inquiry, philosophers may well attempt to analyze some terms which are essential in the philosophical study of language, e.g. 'meaning', 'truth', and 'synonymy'.

One of the basic facts about language is that it is possible to understand a sentence we have never seen before, if we understand the words used to make up the sentence. So philosophers of language have been concerned to investigate the way in which the meaning of words contributes to the meaning of those sentences in which the words are used. In the course of this inquiry, investigation has been made into the logical form of sentences of different kinds—intensional and extensional, for example—in order to clarify the differences in the way words contribute to the meaning of sentences.

The topics discussed in Chapter IV are illustrative of problems in philosophy of language. What is the relation between the sense of a word and its reference? Is the meaning of a word nothing more than its sense and its reference, or are the images a word brings to mind part of its meaning? Some words do not refer to anything in the world—for example, 'Pegasus', 'unicorn', 'centaur'. If the reference of a word is part of its meaning, how can we account for the fact that these words can be used in meaningful sentences? We have spoken of the *use* of words in sentences; philosophers have often discussed the relation between the use of a word and its meaning. An introduction to this discussion is presented in Chapter VII.

A major endeavor in the philosophy of language has

been the search for a formal definition of truth, which neither leads to contradictions nor conflicts with our strong intuition that any sentence 'S' is true if and only if the state of affairs described by 'S' is the case. And it is as much in the philosophy of language as in epistemology that the dispute noted in Chapter VI has been waged, as to whether or not the analytic-synthetic distinction is tenable.

The emphasis in recent years on logic and the analytic method of philosophy has no doubt stimulated interest in the problems of philosophy of language. But like questions in other areas of philosophy, many of those in philosophy of language—such as "What is the meaning of 'truth'?"—have been discussed since the time of Plato and Aristotle.

9. *Philosophy of Mind*

Philosophy of mind, as a separate area of philosophical inquiry, has not played as prominent a role in the history of philosophy as ethics or epistemology. But this is not to say that the problems in this area have only recently come to be discussed. Inquiry into the nature of intentional action, desire, and motivation is present throughout the history of philosophy.

In discussing ethics, we observed that some philosophers have attempted to define the rightness of an action in terms of the motives from which the agent acted. To talk about a person's motives, intentions, desires, or beliefs is to talk about something mental or psychological. In order to gain some insight into the nature of these mental phenomena, philosophers have investigated the logical structure of the sentences used to describe motives, beliefs, and the like. Typically, such sentences are *intensional* (see Chapter V). Some philosophers of mind feel that intensionality is the most important feature of discourse about psychological phenomena, and they have devoted their energies to a detailed study of the logical properties of intensional sentences.

The analysis of the concept of belief is another important problem in this area. Is what a person says about his beliefs to be taken as conclusive evidence of what he believes? The familiar saying that actions speak louder than words finds an analogue in the philosophical argument that what a person does must be taken as the final evidence of what he believes. Others have argued that it is not enough to say that a person's actions are *evidence* of his beliefs (or of his desires or intentions); rather, that these mental notions have no meaning except that which can be defined in terms of a person's behavior or his physical responses to stimuli. Such problems of the relation of mind to body, of the mental to the physical, have played an important role in philosophy, particularly since Descartes.

Closely related to the concepts we have been discussing (i.e. motive, desire, etc.) is the concept of intentional action. So much philosophical inquiry has been focused on this concept in recent years that it would not be amiss to treat "philosophy of action" as a separate field. But to do so would be to de-emphasize the close connection between the problems involved in the analysis of action and other problems in the philosophy of mind.

What is the nature of action? How, for example, can the things a person does be distinguished from the things that happen to him? What is the relation between an action's being intentional and its being voluntary? And further, what is the distinction between a man's *deciding* to do something and his *predicting* that he will do it? All these are questions arising from the attempt to analyze the concept of action.

In addition, philosophers of mind have attempted to clarify the distinction between a person's *reasons* for acting as he does and the *causes* of his action. Are the beliefs, desires, and motives of a person reasons for his actions or causes of it, or both?

It may seem difficult to distinguish the philosopher's task from the psychologist's. But the philosopher is not an empirical scientist. The relations he seeks among the concepts we have referred to are not connections one could discover in a laboratory. The philosopher seeks to make an analysis of such concepts as believing, desiring and intending which will make clear the logical relations between them. For example, most philosophers hold that it is a logical presupposition of a person's intending to do something that he believes it to be possible for him to do it. The philosopher's evidence is not that people usually, or even always, believe that they can do what they intend to do. Rather, his evidence comes from an analysis of the concepts. His claim is that part of what it *means* to intend to do something is that one believes one can do it.

10. *Philosophy of History*

The philosopher of history studies history in much the same way as the philosopher of science studies science. He may ask just what history is, e.g. whether it is essential to history that historians interpret past events or attempt to discover patterns in history. Historians typically attempt to *explain* events and people's actions, and historical explanations have received as much attention from philosophers as have scientific explanations. Are historical explanations *causal* explanations? Are the requirements for an acceptable explanation in history different from those in science? The objects of historical study are primarily human actions and events as they influence and affect people; does this fact influence the kind of explanation which is appropriate? Does an explanation which gives the reasons for a person's action also give the causes? Is it a sufficient explanation for a person's action to give his reasons? What role does the notion of "law" play in history? Are there historical laws at all? Do the criteria for a law in history differ from those in science; is it an historical law that a hungry people is a people bent on revolution?

A philosopher might also investigate the role that historical evidence plays in predictions. Does the logical form of the prediction of an event in the history of man parallel the logical form of a scientific prediction? There seem to be many ways in which the method of historians differs from that of scientists. To ask what history is, is to ask in part whether history is a science. Do the differences between history and science cast doubt on the validity of history as a source of knowledge, or are the differences simply a product of different subject matter?

The question of evidence or good reasons recurs throughout philosophy, and philosophy of history is no exception. Historians often offer theories of history to account for the past, theories which may, for example, purport to show a pattern in past events. If two such theories conflict, what would constitute evidence in favor of either? Does the past itself provide evidence? Events in the past are in principle unobservable; they have already occurred. The philosopher of history shares with the epistemologist an interest in how or whether it is possible to have knowledge of the past. Does memory provide us with evidence about the past, or does the fact that one can believe he remembers something which did not actually occur invalidate evidence from memory?

11. *Philosophy of Religion*

Philosophy of religion is not theology, nor is it a body of religious beliefs; rather it is a critical investigation of the meaning and justification of religious statements. Just as the philosopher may ask what constitutes scientific evidence, he may also ask what constitutes evidence for religious belief. While it is generally agreed, however, that scientific knowledge must be justified by appeal to evidence, it has been asked not only whether there *can* be evidence for religious propositions, but also whether such propositions stand in need of supporting evidence.

Philosophers have inquired into just what kind of propositions the propositions of religion are. If they purport to give information about the world, they are not analytic. But if they are synthetic, on what grounds is one to confirm or deny them? Can revelation be a source of evidence? A distinction has often been made between revealed theology, by which this question is answered affirmatively, and rational or natural theology. Natural theology begins with evidence from the world or nature as we find it; it is said to be rational because its method is that of argument from purported facts about the world to claims about the existence and the nature of a divine being. If this distinction is correctly drawn, is there any reason to hold that one of these kinds of belief is better justified than the other?

Since the Middle Ages, when many philosophers were theologians as well, part of the philosophy or religion has been concerned with purported proofs for the existence of God. Are any proofs possible? The so-called ontological argument purports to deduce God's existence, not from empirical facts, but merely from an analysis of the concept of God. Many other arguments for the existence of God may be offered as well: the argument from design may be based on the claim that God must exist, in order to account for the order in the universe; in giving a causal argument, one may hold that, since everything that exists must have a cause, and the universe exists, then God must exist as the cause of the universe; finally, one may offer a moral argument, to show that only in terms of God's existence can we explain moral values. But each of these arguments is open to serious objections of various sorts. Thus the philosopher of religion may ask whether these arguments can be defended against the objections, modified so as to avoid them, or supplanted by new arguments which are not open to objection.

The question of whether God exists or not is closely related to the question of the nature or attributes of God. If we merely assert that God exists, but refuse to describe His nature, then the assertion of existence can be of no real interest. But if we attempt to describe His nature, then a host of new problems arises. If, for example, God is said to be omniscient, omnipotent and benevolent, then the existence of evil poses a major difficulty. If God is omniscient, He knows about evil; if He is omnipotent, He can eliminate it; if He is benevolent, He opposes evil. Yet evil exists; God must therefore lack one of these three properties of omnipotence, omniscience and benevolence. Such problems are typical of those in the philosophy of religion.

Not all philosophers, of course, have been concerned with statements about a god within the Judaeo-Christian tradition. Some have argued that, while man can prove the existence of a god, it is one that differs significantly from the God of Western tradition. Others claim to be able to prove that no god exists; still others deny the meaningfulness of all claims about the existence of any being which cannot be verified empirically.

12. *Political Philosophy and Philosophy of Law*

Political philosophy consists essentially of inquiry into the relationship between individuals in a governed society and the government of that society. Unlike much of political science, it is not especially concerned with the description and analysis of existing governments. Rather, it is mainly concerned with examining the reasons for having any government at all and considering, in the light of those reasons, the justifiability of various features which governments may have. Thus, the political philosopher is likely to ask what general form the political organization of society should take. In seeking to answer this question, he will be faced with the task of considering the nature of man and the functions and purposes of social organization. Thomas Hobbes, for example, begins his treatise on political philosophy, *The Leviathan,* with a discussion of the nature of man, arguing that, in the absence of political organization, life is "solitary, poor, nasty, brutish, and short," and that it is the function of political organization to provide men with a way of "getting themselves out from that miserable condition." He then goes on to consider, in the light of these views, what form the political organization of society should take.

Once a view of the nature of man and the function of political organization has been accepted, the question of the proper form of government involves many other philosophically interesting issues. What, for example, is the proper relation between law and morality? Some have argued that the body of laws in a society must reflect the moral attitudes which predominate in that society. Others hold that morality is essentially outside the law, and that consequently it is inappropriate for legislation to be concerned with matters of morality at all. Rather, they argue, law results from an attempt by organized society to limit individual or group freedom, only in so far as its unrestricted exercise would injure individuals or groups within the society.

A related question, which is equally basic, concerns the procedure within the state for establishing and changing laws. When an individual is a member of a governed society, he is, it seems, committed to abide by its laws. What, then, are the rights and obligations of the citizen who considers a law to be unjustifiable? One can argue, for example, that it was wrong for citizens of Nazi Germany to obey Hitler's genocidal laws. But on what grounds was it wrong? Is it because obedience to those laws was a violation of some natural law? Such is the view that some philosophers have held. But then the question of the possibility of natural law must be considered, and new problems arise when we ask how natural laws, if there can be any, are discoverable.

Such questions about the nature and function of political organization are obviously inseparable from questions about the nature and function of laws. Hence there can be no complete division between political philosophy and philosophy of law. There are differences nonetheless. Philosophy of law, for example, is concerned to a large degree with philosophical issues connected with particular bodies of law or with the concept of law within a particular legal tradition. Thus, most philosophers of law in English-speaking countries are concerned with those questions that relate especially to the Anglo-American legal tradition.

Many of these questions are closely connected with problems in ethics, particularly those concerning the responsibility of agents. Systems of law as we know them rely on the notion of an agent's being responsible for his action. This is clearly revealed by the fact that we regard as relevant to the guilt of an accused person testimony as to whether or not he was under compulsion to act as he did. Two sets of questions naturally arise at this point. First, what does it mean to say that a person is or is not responsible? Is there, for instance, a difference between moral and legal responsibility? If so, what is the relationship between them? If not, how can we account for our conviction that justice and legality can sometimes fail to coincide?

Second, in what way does a person's lack of responsibility excuse him from blame or guilt, assuming that he did in fact perform the action in question? Such a question leads naturally to consideration of causality. For if we are to consider the consequences of an action in evaluating it, we must first be able to tell when a person's action is the cause of a subsequent event.

Further questions in philosophy of law also raise issues in other areas of philosophy. If, for example, we wish to hold that certain promises become binding contracts, we must be able to decide what is involved in the making of a promise. But what constitutes promising is a question in ethics and philosophy of language. And if we wish to count the intentions and motives of an agent as relevant in evaluating his action, this will lead us to consider what constitutes evidence about the mental state of another, what is involved in performing an act voluntarily, and what the connection is between freedom of the will and responsibility. These are paradigmatic questions of epistemology, philosophy of mind, and ethics.

13. History of Philosophy

The distinctions we have thus far suggested within the body of philosophy have been based on typical

questions from each area. However, one may also regard philosophy through its chronological development, in the study of the history of philosophy. It is
difficult to say exactly what constitutes an historical
study of philosophy. If, for example, one were to study
what philosophers during the seventeenth and eighteenth centuries wrote about epistemological questions,
he would soon become involved in criticism and evaluation—that is, in epistemological inquiry. Yet he is also
engaged in an historical study. And any purported
epistemological study which does not take cognizance
of the writings of past philosophers is simply not a
thorough study. The problems of philosophy have not
changed as much as, e.g. those of science; therefore,
attention to past writings is not as peripheral to contemporary philosophy as it often is to contemporary
science. In this sense, there is always reason for attention to history in philosophy.

One approach to an historical study of philosophy is,
as we have mentioned above, to study those writings
from a particular period of time that are concerned
with selected problems. But many other approaches
are possible. One can also study the writings of some
one philosopher about many problems. In so doing,
one may be interested in the effect that the philosopher's metaphysical arguments have had on his epistemological or ethical position. Are the positions he takes
on various questions consistent with one another? Do
his metaphysical presuppositions conflict with his epistemological claims? In the course of such an inquiry it
may be useful to classify a philosopher as, for example,
a materialist or an idealist, a rationalist or an empiri-
cist. Such classification is no end in itself, of course, but
it may provide insight into the influence that previous
philosophers have had on a writer and into his influence on subsequent writers. It must be kept in mind

that when we say that two philosophers are, for example, empiricists, we are saying that in some respects their positions are alike. But it is just as important to recognize the respects in which their positions differ.

Philosophers have never lived in a vacuum; their writings have always been influenced by the writings of other philosophers, as well as by the society in which they live. It is often useful to study one philosopher in the light of some preceding philosophical writings of which he takes cognizance in his writings. In this way, one may come to have a clearer grasp of the problems to which the philosopher has addressed himself, and may thus be better able to understand his writings. An historian of philosophy is often interested in the fact that problems of a particular kind predominate in the writings of a given period. For example, Greek philosophy before Socrates was primarily concerned to discover the fundamental stuff of which the universe was composed. But with the philosophy of Socrates came a notable change in focus from man's environment to man himself, and his relations to other men. To a philosopher, the questions that have been asked in philosophy are often as interesting as the answers that have been given.

14. Conclusion

Two points must be emphasized about the divisions within the body of philosophy. First, the areas are not independent of one another; rarely is any study in philosophy irrelevant to any other study in philosophy. Arguments in one area may be presupposed by the discussion of a problem, or even its formulation, in another. If, in the philosophy of science, one is investigating different methods for the confirmation of theories, he must have in mind some criterion for the adequacy of evidence. He may even attack his problem by first attempting to discover the epistemological assumptions of various methods of confirmation.

Second, the demarcation of areas in philosophy is neither an exhaustive nor an unchanging classification. It is often neither possible nor important to decide to what area of inquiry a particular question belongs. Is the question of the tenability of the analytic-synthetic distinction an epistemological question, or one for the philosophy of language? This question is moot, but inquiry into the analytic-synthetic distinction in no way presupposes any answer to this question. Some questions in philosophy underlie several specific studies: the question of the logical structure of explanations is as relevant to the philosophy of science as it is to the philosophy of history. And specific studies of historical and scientific explanations in turn shed light on the more general question of the nature of explanation.

This chapter will have served the purpose for which it was intended if the reader has gained from it some insight into the general problems to which philosophers have addressed themselves, and is thereby better able to understand his readings in philosophy.

Bibliography

The following is a list of books and series which are of major importance in the development of analytic philosophy or are particularly helpful to the introductory student. All are by contemporary British and American authors. No attempt has been made to provide an exhaustive bibliography of contemporary analytic philosophy, nor are any books included which were written prior to the twentieth century or outside the current Anglo–American philosophical tradition.

The branches of philosophy to which each work listed is primarily relevant are indicated by capital letters following each entry according to the following code: A—anthology; B—series; C—philosophy of language; D—metaphysics; E—epistemology; F—philosophy of science; G—ethics and theory of value; H—aesthetics; I—philosophy of law; J—philosophy of religion; K—philosophy of history; L—logic and philosophy of logic; M—philosophy of mind; N—history of philosophy.

1. Anscombe, G. E. M. *Intention.* 2d ed.; Oxford: Basil Blackwell, 1963. (E, G, M)
2. Anscombe, G. E. M., and P. T. Geach. *Three Philosophers.* Oxford: Basil Blackwell, 1961. (D, L, N)
3. Armstrong, D. M. *Perception and the Physical World.* New York: The Humanities Press, 1961. (See number 7.) (E, M)
4. Austin, J. L. *How to Do Things with Words.* Cambridge, Mass.: Harvard University Press, 1962. (C)

5. Austin, J. L. *Philosophical Papers*. Oxford: Clarendon Press, 1961. (C)
6. Austin, J. L. *Sense and Sensibilia*. Oxford: Clarendon Press, 1962. (E)
   Paperback: New York: Oxford University Press, 1964 (Galaxy Books).
7. Ayer, A. J., editor. INTERNATIONAL LIBRARY OF PHILOSOPHY AND SCIENTIFIC METHOD. London: Routledge and Kegan Paul; New York: The Humanities Press. (B)
8. Ayer, A. J. *Language, Truth and Logic*. 2d ed.; London: V. Gollancz, 1946. (C, D, E, G, L)
   Paperback: New York: Dover Publications, Inc., 1952.
9. Ayer, A. J. *The Problem of Knowledge*. New York: St. Martin's Press, 1956. (E, M)
   Paperback: Baltimore: Penguin Books, 1962.
10. Beardsley, Elizabeth and Monroe Beardsley, editors. THE PRENTICE-HALL FOUNDATIONS OF PHILOSOPHY SERIES (paperback series). Englewood Cliffs, N.J.: Prentice-Hall, Inc.
    Aldrich, Virgil. *Philosophy of Art*
    Alston, William. *Philosophy of Language*
    Banker, Stephen. *Philosophy of Mathematics*
    Chisholm, Roderick. *Theory of Knowledge*
    Dray, William. *Philosophy of History*
    Frankena, William. *Ethics*
    Hempel, Carl. *Philosophy of Natural Science*
    Hick, John. *Philosophy of Religion*
    Hook, Sidney. *Political Philosophy*
    Lenz, John. *Philosophy of Education*
    Rudner, Richard. *Philosophy of Social Science*
    Salmon, Wesley. *Logic*
    Taylor, Richard. *Metaphysics*
11. Bird, Graham. *Kant's Theory of Knowledge*. New York: The Humanities Press, 1962. (See number 7.) (D, E, M, N)
12. Black, Max, editor. CONTEMPORARY PHILOSOPHY. Ithaca, N.Y.: Cornell University Press. (B)
13. Black, Max. *Problems of Analysis*. Ithaca, N.Y.: Cornell University Press, 1954. (A)
14. Broad, C. D. *Five Types of Ethical Theory*. London: Routledge and Kegan Paul, 1930. (See number 60.) (G, N)
    Paperback: Paterson, N.J.: Littlefield, Adams & Co., 1959.
15. Butler, R. J., editor. *Analytical Philosophy*. New York: Barnes and Noble, 1963. (A)
16. Castaneda, H.-N., and G. Nakhnikian, editors. *Morality*

and the Language of Conduct. Detroit: Wayne State University Press, 1963. (A, G)

17. Caton, Charles Edwin, editor. *Philosophy and Ordinary Language.* Urbana: University of Illinois Press, 1963 (paperback). (A, C)

18. Chappell, V. C., editor. *Ordinary Language.* Englewood Cliffs, N.J.: Prentice-Hall, Inc., 1964. (See number 27.) (A, C)

19. Chappell, V. C., editor. *The Philosophy of Mind.* Englewood Cliffs, N.J.: Prentice-Hall, Inc., 1962 (paperback). (A, M)

20. Chisholm, Roderick M. *Perceiving.* Ithaca, N.Y.: Cornell University Press, 1957. (See number 12.) (E, G)

21. Danto, Arthur, and Sidney Morgenbesser, editors. *Philosophy of Science.* New York: Meridian Books, 1960 (paperback). (A, F)

22. Dray, William. *Laws and Explanation in History.* London: Oxford University Press, 1957. (F, K)

23. Elton, William, editor. *Aesthetics and Language.* Oxford: Basil Blackwell, 1954. (A, H)

24. Feigl, Herbert, *et al.*, editors. MINNESOTA STUDIES IN THE PHILOSOPHY OF SCIENCE. Minneapolis: University of Minnesota Press. (A, B)

25. Feigl, Herbert, and Wilfred Sellars, editors. *Readings in Philosophical Analysis.* New York: Appleton-Century-Crofts, 1949. (A)

26. Feigl, Herbert, and May Brodbeck, editors. *Readings in the Philosophy of Science.* New York: Appleton-Century-Crofts, 1953. (A, F)

27. Feinberg, Joel, and Wesley C. Salmon, editors. CONTEMPORARY PERSPECTIVES IN PHILOSOPHY (paperback series). Englewood Cliffs, N.J.: Prentice-Hall, Inc. (B)

28. Flew, Antony G. N., editor. *Essays in Conceptual Analysis.* London: Macmillan & Co., 1956. (A, C, D, E, F, L)

29. Flew, Antony G. N., editor. *Logic and Language* (First series). Oxford: Basil Blackwell, 1952. (A)

30. Flew, Antony G. N., editor. *Logic and Language* (Second series). Oxford: Basil Blackwell, 1953. (A)

31. Flew, Antony G. N. *Hume's Philosophy of Belief.* New York: The Humanities Press, 1961. (See number 7.) (D, E, J, M, N)

32. Flew, Antony G. N., and Alasdair MacIntyre, editors. *New Essays in Philosophical Theology.* London: SCM Press, 1955. (A, D, J)

33. Fodor, Jerry, and Jerrold Katz, editors. *Philosophy of Language.* Englewood Cliffs, N.J.: Prentice-Hall, Inc., 1964. (A, C)

34. Gardiner, Patrick, editor. *Theories of History*. Glencoe, Ill.: The Free Press, 1959. (A, K)
35. Goodman, Nelson. *Fact, Fiction and Forecast*. Cambridge, Mass.: Harvard University Press, 1955. (D, E, F)
36. Hare, R. M. *Freedom and Reason*. Oxford: Clarendon Press, 1963. (G)
37. Hare, R. M. *The Language of Morals*. Oxford: Clarendon Press, 1952. (G)
    Paperback: New York: Oxford University Press, 1964 (Galaxy Books).
38. Hart, H. L. A. *The Concept of Law*. Oxford: Clarendon Press, 1961. (I)
39. Hart, H. L. A., and A. M. Honore. *Causation in the Law*. Oxford: Clarendon Press, 1959. (D, F, I)
40. Hempel, Carl G. *Fundamentals of Concept Formation in Empirical Science*. Chicago: The University of Chicago Press, 1952. (See number 59.) (F)
41. Holland, R. F., editor. STUDIES IN PHILOSOPHICAL PSYCHOLOGY. London: Routledge and Kegan Paul; New York: The Humanities Press. (B)
42. Hospers, John. *An Introduction to Philosophical Analysis*. Englewood Cliffs, N.J.: Prentice-Hall, Inc., 1963. (E, G)
43. Katz, Joseph, *et al.*, editors. *Writers on Ethics*. Princeton, N.J.: D. Van Nostrand Co., Inc., 1962. (A, G)
44. Kaufmann, Walter Arnold. *Critique of Religion and Philosophy*. New York: Harper, 1958. (G, J)
    Paperback: Garden City, N.Y.: Anchor Books, 1961.
45. Kenny, Anthony. *Action, Emotion and Will*. London: Routledge and Kegan Paul, 1963. (See number 41.) (E, G, M)
46. Kuhn, Thomas S. *The Structure of Scientific Revolutions*. Chicago: The University of Chicago Press, 1962. (See number 59.) (F)
47. Kyburg, Henry E., Jr., and Howard E. Smokler, editors. *Studies in Subjective Probability*. New York: John Wiley & Sons, Inc., 1964 (paperback). (A, F)
48. Lazerowitz, Morris. *The Structure of Metaphysics*. London: Routledge and Kegan Paul, 1953. (See number 60.) (D, E)
49. Lewis, C. I. *Mind and the World Order*. New York: Scribner, 1929. (D, E)
    Paperback: New York: Dover Publications, Inc., 1956.
50. MacDonald, Margaret, editor. *Philosophy and Analysis*. Oxford: Basil Blackwell, 1954. (A)
51. Madden, Edward H. *The Structure of Scientific Thought*. Boston: Houghton Mifflin, 1960. (F)
52. Margolis, Joseph, editor. *Philosophy Looks at the Arts*. New York: Charles Scribner's Sons, 1964 (paperback). (A, H)

53. Melden, A. I., editor. *Essays in Moral Philosophy*. Seattle: University of Washington Press, 1958. (A, G)
54. Melden, A. I., editor. *Ethical Theories*. 2d ed.; Englewood Cliffs, N.J.: Prentice-Hall, Inc., 1961. (A, G)
55. Moore, G. E. *Principia Ethica*. Cambridge: Cambridge University Press, 1903. (G)
   Paperback: Cambridge: Cambridge University Press, 1962.
56. Morgenbesser, Sidney, and James Walsh, editors. *Free Will*. Englewood Cliffs, N.J.: Prentice-Hall, Inc., 1962 (paperback). (A, G, M)
57. Morris, Herbert, editor. *Freedom and Responsibility*. Stanford: Stanford University Press, 1961. (A, G, I)
58. Nagel, Ernest. *Principles of the Theory of Probability*. Chicago: University of Chicago Press, 1939. (See number 59.) (F)
59. Neurath, Otto, Rudolf Carnap, and Charles Morris, editors. INTERNATIONAL ENCYCLOPEDIA OF UNIFIED SCIENCE. Chicago: The University of Chicago Press. (B)
60. Ogden, C. K., editor. INTERNATIONAL LIBRARY OF PHILOSOPHY, PSYCHOLOGY, AND SCIENTIFIC METHOD. London: Routledge and Kegan Paul. (B)
61. Pap, Arthur. *Elements of Analytic Philosophy*. New York: Macmillan, 1949.
62. Pap, Arthur. *An Introduction to the Philosophy of Science*. New York: The Free Press of Glencoe, 1962. (E, F)
63. Passmore, John A. *A Hundred Years of Philosophy*. London: G. Duckworth, 1957. (N)
64. Pears, D. F., editor. *Freedom and the Will*. New York: St. Martin's Press, 1963. (A, D, G, I, M)
65. Pitcher, George, editor. *Truth*. Englewood Cliffs, N.J.: Prentice-Hall, Inc., 1964. (See number 27.) (A, C, L)
66. Quine, Willard Van Orman. *From a Logical Point of View*. 2d ed. rev.; Cambridge, Mass.: Harvard University Press, 1961. (C, D, L)
   Paperback: New York: Harper Torchbooks, 1963.
67. Quine, Willard Van Orman. *Methods of Logic*. 2d ed. rev.; New York: Henry Holt and Company, 1959. (L)
68. Quine, Willard Van Orman. *Word and Object*. New York: John Wiley & Sons, Inc., 1960. (C, D, E, L, M)
69. Rader, Melvin. *A Modern Book of Esthetics*. 3d ed. rev.; New York: Holt, Rinehart and Winston, Inc., 1960. (A, H)
70. Russell, Bertrand. *Introduction to Mathematical Philosophy*. London: George Allen & Unwin, Ltd., 1919. (L)
71. Russell, Bertrand. *The Problems of Philosophy*. New York: Henry Holt and Company, 1912. (D, E)

Paperback: New York: Oxford University Press, 1959 (Galaxy Books).

72. Ryle, Gilbert. *The Concept of Mind.* London: Hutchison's University Library, 1949. (F, M)
   Paperback: New York: Barnes and Noble, 1962.

73. Ryle, Gilbert. *Dilemmas.* Cambridge: Cambridge University Press, 1954. (C, D, M)
   Paperback: Cambridge: Cambridge University Press, 1959.

74. Scheffler, Israel. *The Anatomy of Inquiry.* New York: Alfred A. Knopf, Inc., 1963. (E, F)

75. Schilpp, Paul Arthur, editor. THE LIBRARY OF LIVING PHILOSOPHERS. La Salle, Ill.: Open Court; London: Cambridge University Press. (B)

76. Sellars, Wilfred, and John Hospers, editors. *Readings in Ethical Theory.* New York: Appleton-Century-Crofts, 1952. (A, G)

77. Sidgwick, Henry. *Outlines of the History of Ethics.* 6th ed. enl.; London: Macmillan, 1954. (G, N)
   Paperback: Boston: Beacon Paperbacks, 1962.

78. Singer, Marcus George. *Generalization in Ethics.* New York: Alfred A. Knopf, Inc., 1961. (G)

79. Stevenson, Charles L. *Ethics and Language.* New Haven: Yale University Press, 1944. (C, G)
   Paperback: New Haven: Yale University Press, 1960.

80. Strawson, P. F. *Individuals; An Essay in Descriptive Metaphysics.* London: Methuen, 1959. (C, D, L, M)
   Paperback: Garden City, N.Y.: Anchor Books, 1963.

81. Suppes, Patrick. *Introduction to Logic.* Princeton, N.J.: D. Van Nostrand Co., 1957. (L)

82. Toulmin, Stephen. *An Examination of the Place of Reason in Ethics.* Cambridge: Cambridge University Press, 1953. (F, G, J)
   Paperback: Cambridge: Cambridge University Press, 1961.

83. Urmson, J. O. *Philosophical Analysis.* Oxford: Clarendon Press, 1958. (C, D, E, L, N)

84. Vivas, Eliseo, and Murray Krieger, editors. *The Problems of Aesthetics.* New York: Rinehart, 1953. (A, H)

85. Warnock, G. J. *Berkeley.* Baltimore: Penguin Books, 1953 (paperback). (C, E, J, M, N)

86. Warnock, Mary. *Ethics Since 1900.* London: Oxford University Press, 1960. (G, N)

87. Wasserstrom, Richard Alan. *The Judicial Decision.* Stanford: Stanford University Press, 1961. (I)

88. Wilder, Raymond L. *Introduction to the Foundations of Mathematics.* New York: John Wiley and Sons, Inc., 1952. (L)

89. Wittgenstein, Ludwig. *Philosophical Investigations*. Translated by G. E. M. Anscombe. New York: The Macmillan Company, 1953. (C, D, E, F, G, H, L, M)
90. Wright, Georg Henrik von. *The Varieties of Goodness*. New York: The Humanities Press, 1963. (See number 7.) (G, M)

Index

STUDIES IN PHILOSOPHY

STUDIES IN PSYCHOLOGY

STUDIES IN POLITICAL SCIENCE

STUDIES IN SOCIOLOGY